Blockchain for Ente

Build scalable blockchain applications with privacy, interoperability, and permissioned features

Narayan Prusty

BIRMINGHAM - MUMBAI

Blockchain for Enterprise

Commissioning Editor: Sunith Shetty
Acquisition Editor: Namrata Patil
Content Development Editor: Chris D'cruz
Technical Editor: Suwarna Patil
Copy Editor: Safis Editing
Project Coordinator: Nidhi Joshi
Proofreader: Safis Editing
Indexer: Tejal Daruwale Soni
Graphics: Tom Scaria
Production Coordinator: Nilesh Mohite

First published: September 2018
Production reference: 1250918

Published by Packt Publishing Ltd.
Livery Place
35 Livery Street
Birmingham
B3 2PB, UK.

ISBN 978-1-78847-974-5

www.packtpub.com

`mapt.io`

Mapt is an online digital library that gives you full access to over 5,000 books and videos, as well as industry leading tools to help you plan your personal development and advance your career. For more information, please visit our website.

Why subscribe?

- Spend less time learning and more time coding with practical eBooks and Videos from over 4,000 industry professionals

- Improve your learning with Skill Plans built especially for you

- Get a free eBook or video every month

- Mapt is fully searchable

- Copy and paste, print, and bookmark content

packt.com

Did you know that Packt offers eBook versions of every book published, with PDF and ePub files available? You can upgrade to the eBook version at `www.packt.com` and as a print book customer, you are entitled to a discount on the eBook copy. Get in touch with us at `customercare@packtpub.com` for more details.

At `www.packt.com`, you can also read a collection of free technical articles, sign up for a range of free newsletters, and receive exclusive discounts and offers on Packt books and eBooks.

Contributors

About the author

Narayan Prusty is the founder and CTO of BlockCluster, world's first blockchain management system. He has five years of experience in blockchain. He specializes in Blockchain, DevOps, Serverless, and JavaScript. His commitment has led him to build scalable products for start-ups, governments, and enterprises across India, Singapore, USA, and UAE. He is enthusiastic about solving real-world problems. His ability to build scalable applications from top to bottom is what makes him special. Currently, he is on a mission to make things easier, faster, and cheaper using blockchain. Also, he is looking at ways to prevent corruption, fraud, and to bring transparency to the world using blockchain.

About the reviewers

Nikhil Bhaskar is the founder and CEO of Ulixir Inc—a newly founded tech company that builds decentralized and traditional software. He completed B9lab's Ethereum Developer Course, and he is now a certified Ethereum developer. Aside from running Ulixir, he spends his time traveling and eating. He is a bit of a digital nomad; this year, he's lived in five countries and plans to live in six more before the year ends.

Ivan Turkovic is a geek, visionary, start-up enthusiast, writer, blogger, mentor, and advisor. He wrote the book *PhoneGap Essentials*. Since 2011 he has had a strong interest in Bitcoin and blockchain. In 2013 he co-founded a social start-up, Babberly, which was among the first to use gamification with the help of blockchain.

He is focused on bringing value to the internet users. He employs the latest technologies to build empowering web products and intuitive user experiences. He's interested in technology, entrepreneurship, education, behavior psychology, product management, and marketing. He runs Blaeg, a company that helps start-ups get off the ground with their blockchain technology.

Anand V. is a technology architect who has more than 20 years of experience in IT. He has worked with Verizon Communications, Cognizant, HP, HCL, and Oracle. Currently, he is the managing partner of Anasup Consulting and works with clients on emerging technologies such as blockchain, IoT, cybersecurity, and AI. He is also a specialist in the DevSecOps area and acts as a mentor to many start-up companies. He is a public speaker and regularly writes articles in journals as well as online channels.

Packt is searching for authors like you

If you're interested in becoming an author for Packt, please visit authors.packtpub.com and apply today. We have worked with thousands of developers and tech professionals, just like you, to help them share their insight with the global tech community. You can make a general application, apply for a specific hot topic that we are recruiting an author for, or submit your own idea.

Table of Contents

Preface

Blockchain is growing massively, and is changing the way that business is done. Leading organizations are already exploring the possibilities of blockchain. With this book, you will learn how to build end-to-end, enterprise-level **decentralized applications (DApps)** and scale them across your organization to meet your company's needs.

This book will help you understand what DApps are and the workings of the blockchain ecosystem with some real-world examples. This is an extensive end-to-end book covering every aspect of blockchain, such as its applications for businesses and developers. It will help you be aware of the process flows so you can incorporate them into your own enterprise. You will learn how to use J.P. Morgan's Quorum to build blockchain-based applications. You will also be introduced to how to write applications that can help communicate in enterprise blockchain solutions. You will learn how to write smart contracts that run without censorship and third-party interference.

Once you have a good grip on what blockchain is and have learned all about Quorum, you will jump into building real-world practical blockchain applications for sectors such as payment and money transfer, healthcare, cloud computing, supply chain management, and much more.

Who this book is for

This book is for innovators, digital transformers, and blockchain developers who want to build end-to-end DApps using blockchain technology. If you want to scale your existing blockchain system across the enterprise, you will find this book useful too. It gives you the practical approach needed for solving real problems in an enterprise using a blend of theory- and practice-based approaches.

What this book covers

Chapter 1, *What are Decentralized Applications?*, will explain what DApps are and provide an overview of blockchain-based DApps.

Chapter 2, *Building Blockchain Using Quorum*, introduces the basics of Ethereum blockchain and the features of Quorum. This chapter also teaches you how to set up a Raft network using Quorum and various third-party tools and libraries.

Chapter 3, *Writing Smart Contracts*, shows how to write smart contracts and use geth's interactive console to deploy and broadcast transactions using web3.js.

Chapter 4, *Getting Started with web3.js*, introduces web3.js and how to import and connect to geth, and explains how to use it in Node.js or client-side JavaScript.

Chapter 5, *Building Interoperable Blockchains*, explores what interoperable blockchains can achieve, the various technologies and patterns for achieving blockchain interoperability, and building interoperable blockchain networks to represent FedCoins.

Chapter 6, *Building Quorum as a Service Platform* , will teach you the basics of cloud computing and containerization by examples. You'll learn how to install minikube, deploy containers on Kubernetes, and develop a Quorum-as-a-service using QNM.

Chapter 7, *Building a DApps for Digitizing Medical Records* , gets into how to use proxy re-encryption to enable encrypted data sharing in blockchain. Besides proxy re-encryption, you'll also learn about a lot of JavaScript and Python libraries, such as `etherumjs-wallet`, `ethereumjs-tx`, `ethereumjs-util`, and `npre`. Also, you'll learn about signing transactions using keys stored outside a geth node.

Chapter 8, *Building a Payment Solution for Banks*, looks at how to implement network permissioning in Quorum and how to build a solution to transfer money using a mobile number.

To get the most out of this book

You must have experience with the JavaScript and Python programming languages.

You must have developed distributed web applications before.

You must understand the basic cryptography concepts, such as signing, encryption, and hashing.

Download the example code files

You can download the example code files for this book from your account at `www.packt.com`. If you purchased this book elsewhere, you can visit `www.packt.com/support` and register to have the files emailed directly to you.

You can download the code files by following these steps:

1. Log in or register at www.packt.com.
2. Select the **SUPPORT** tab.
3. Click on **Code Downloads & Errata**.
4. Enter the name of the book in the **Search** box and follow the onscreen instructions.

Once the file is downloaded, please make sure that you unzip or extract the folder using the latest version of:

- WinRAR/7-Zip for Windows
- Zipeg/iZip/UnRarX for Mac
- 7-Zip/PeaZip for Linux

The code bundle for the book is also hosted on GitHub at https://github.com/PacktPublishing/Blockchain-for-Enterprise. In case there's an update to the code, it will be updated on the existing GitHub repository.

We also have other code bundles from our rich catalog of books and videos available at https://github.com/PacktPublishing/. Check them out!

Conventions used

There are a number of text conventions used throughout this book.

CodeInText: Indicates code words in text, database table names, folder names, filenames, file extensions, pathnames, dummy URLs, user input, and Twitter handles. Here is an example: "This Raft ID will appear while adding a node using raft.addPeer."

A block of code is set as follows:

```
url = "http://127.0.0.1:9002/"
port = 9002
storage = "dir:./cnode_data/cnode2/"
socket = "./cnode_data/cnode1/constellation_node2.ipc"
othernodes = ["http://127.0.0.1:9001/"]
publickeys = ["./cnode2.pub"]
privatekeys = ["./cnode2.key"]
tls = "off"
```

Any command-line input or output is written as follows:

```
git clone https://github.com/jpmorganchase/quorum.git
cd quorum
make all
```

Bold: Indicates a new term, an important word, or words that you see onscreen. For example, words in menus or dialog boxes appear in the text like this. Here is an example: "Now select a file, enter the owner's name, and click on **Submit.** ."

 Warnings or important notes appear like this.

 Tips and tricks appear like this.

Get in touch

Feedback from our readers is always welcome.

General feedback: Email `customercare@packtpub.com` and mention the book title in the subject of your message. If you have questions about any aspect of this book, please email us at `customercare@packtpub.com`.

Errata: Although we have taken every care to ensure the accuracy of our content, mistakes do happen. If you have found a mistake in this book, we would be grateful if you would report this to us. Please visit `www.packt.com/submit-errata`, selecting your book, clicking on the Errata Submission Form link, and entering the details.

Piracy: If you come across any illegal copies of our works in any form on the Internet, we would be grateful if you would provide us with the location address or website name. Please contact us at `copyright@packt.com` with a link to the material.

If you are interested in becoming an author: If there is a topic that you have expertise in and you are interested in either writing or contributing to a book, please visit `authors.packtpub.com`.

Reviews

Please leave a review. Once you have read and used this book, why not leave a review on the site that you purchased it from? Potential readers can then see and use your unbiased opinion to make purchase decisions, we at Packt can understand what you think about our products, and our authors can see your feedback on their book. Thank you!

For more information about Packt, please visit `packt.com`.

1
What are Decentralized Applications?

Since the beginning of internet, all internet-based applications that have been developed have been based on client-server architecture, where there is a centralized server that forms the backend of the application and controls the complete application. These applications often end up with issues such as having a single point of failure, failure to prevent net censorship, lack of transparency, users not trusting their data, activity and identity privacy, and so on. This centralized architecture even made it impossible to build certain kinds of applications. For example, you cannot build a digital currency using this architecture. Due to these issues, a new kind of architecture emerged called **Decentralized Applications (DApps)**. In this chapter, we will learn about DApps.

In this chapter, we'll cover the following topics:

- What are DApps?
- What is the difference between decentralized, centralized, and distributed applications?
- What is a blockchain?
- What is the difference between public and permissioned DApps?
- Examples of some of the popular consortium DApps, and how they work
- What are the various popular platforms on which to build enterprise DApps?

What is a DApp?

A DApp is a kind of application whose backend runs on a decentralized peer-to-peer network, and its source code is open source. No single node in the network has complete control of the DApp. Remember that, when we say that an application is decentralized we mean technically it's decentralized but the governance can be distributed, decentralized, or centralized.

The major advantages of DApps are that they don't have a single point of failure, and prevent censorship. DApps do have some disadvantages: it's difficult to fix bugs or add features once deployed as everyone in the network has to update their node software, and it's very complicated to couple different DApps together as they are very difficult to build compared to centralized applications and involve very complex protocols.

To be able to use a DApp, you first need the DApp's node server running so that you can connect to the peer-to-peer network. Then, you need a client respective to the DApp that connects to the node server and exposes a UI or command line interface to use the DApp.

Currently, DApps are not yet as mature as centralized applications in terms of performance and scalability. There is still a lot of research and development on these topics such as performance, scalability, users identity, privacy, communication between DApps, data redundancy, and so on. A use case may fit into a DApp, but whether the use case can be made production-ready with the currently available technology can be a challenge. Popular examples of decentralized applications are Torrent, Bitcoin, Ethereum, Quorum, and so on.

A DApp can be public or permissioned. Public DApps are those which anyone can be part of, in other words, they are permissionless, whereas permissioned DApps are those which are not open for everyone to join, so you will need permission to join. A permissioned DApp is called a **consortium DApp** when the participants of the DApp are enterprises and/or government entities. Similarly, when the participants of a permissioned DApp are only enterprises, then we can call it an enterprise DApp. In this book we will learn everything about permissioned DApps.

 As you just got a basic introduction to what decentralized applications are, you must be wondering what the difference between decentralized and distributed applications is. Well, an application is said to be distributed when it's spread across multiple servers. Decentralized applications are by default distributed, whereas centralized applications may or may not be distributed. Centralized applications are usually distributed across multiple servers to prevent downtime, and also to handle huge data and traffic.

What is a blockchain?

Before we get into what a is, we need to understand what a ledger is. A ledger in computer science is software that stores transactions. A database is different from a ledger such that in a database we can add, remove, and modify records, whereas in a ledger we can only append but not delete or modify.

A blockchain is basically a data structure to implement a decentralized ledger. A blockchain is a chain of blocks connected to each other. Every block contains a list of transactions and certain other metadata, such as when it was created, which is it's previous block, the block number, who is the creator of the block, and so on. Every block maintains a hash of the previous block, therefore creating a chain of blocks linked with each other. Every node in the network should hold the complete copy of the blockchain and, when a new node comes in, it will request and download the blockchain from other nodes.

 Technologies such as blockchains are called **Distributed Ledger Technology (DLT)**. A DLT is the process of replicating, sharing, and synchronizing digital transactions geographically stretched across numerous sites, countries, and/or institutions. You can think of a blockchain as a type of DLT. Also, not every DLT system has to be decentralized. In this book, we only learn to build decentralized blockchain-based applications.

The major advantages of using a blockchain is that it enables the facilitation of transactions without a central trusted party; data is secured using cryptography, and data is immutable, as blockchain removes friction and reduces risk so settlements happen in real time, and so on. Basically, it automates auditing, makes the application transparent, and provides a single source of truth.

In the real world, private blockchains are used in trade finance, cross-border payments, digital identity, the clearing and settlement of tokenized and digital assets, provenance of ownership of a product, record keeping for critical data, signing contracts, multi-party aggregation (namely, they can be used as a shared master repository for common industry information, allowing members to query for data), payment-versus-payment or payment-versus-delivery, and so on.

Every blockchain node maintains a database that contains the blockchain's state. The state contains the final result of running all the transactions in the blockchain. For example, in a blockchain, the state represents the final balances of all addresses. So when you query the blockchain node for an addresses balance, it doesn't have to go through all transactions and calculate the final balance of the address; instead, it directly fetches the balance from the state of the blockchain. Bitcoin uses LevelDB to maintain the state of the blockchain. Even if the database gets corrupted, the database can be restored by simply running all the transactions in the blockchain.

Understanding Byzantine Fault Tolerance

Byzantine Fault Tolerance (BFT) is a characteristic of a decentralized system that indicates that it can tolerate Byzantine failures. A crash failure is when nodes just stopping to do anything (no messages at all) and Byzantine failure is when nodes just don't do anything or exhibit arbitrary behavior. Basically, Byzantine failures include crash failures.

In any decentralized computing environment where a blockchain data structure is used, there is a risk that one or more rogue or unreliable actors could be a reason for the environment to disband. A server cluster will not work well if a few servers within it lose out on passing data to other servers in a consistent manner. In order to be reliable, the decentralized computing environment has to be designed in a way that it has solutions to these kinds of Byzantine failures.

On blockchain-based decentralised applications, there is, by definition, no central authority, so a special kind of protocol called the **consensus protocol** is used to achieve BFT.

In simple terms, you must be wondering how to ensure that everyone has the same copy of the blockchain, and how to know which blockchain is correct when two nodes publish different blockchains? Also, how do you decide who creates the blocks, as there is nothing such as a master node in decentralized architecture? Well, consensus protocols provide an answer to these questions. A few examples of consensus protocols are **Proof-of-Work (PoW)**, **Proof-of-Stake (PoS)**, **Proof-of-Authority (PoA)**, PBFT, and so on.

A consensus protocol is designed specially for permissioned or public blockchains. A consensus protocol made for a public blockchain is likely to create security and performance issues when implemented in a permissioned blockchain. Every consensus protocol has different performance and scalability vectors. You have to be alert while selecting a consensus protocol for your blockchain-based DApp.

 Consensus protocols such as Raft and Paxos are not BFT; rather, they make the system only crash-tolerant. So, you should also consider this when choosing a consensus protocol.

You might have come across the term PoA. PoA is a categorisation of consensus protocols in which there is a set of authorities—nodes that are explicitly allowed to create new blocks and secure the blockchain. Ripple's iterative process, PBFT, Clique, Aura, and so on, are examples of PoA-based consensus protocols.

Representation of user accounts

In blockchain-based applications, user accounts are identified and authenticated using asymmetric key pairs. The private key is used to sign transactions on behalf of the user. Username and password-based accounts systems will not work in blockchain as it cannot be used to prove which user has sent a transaction. The demerits in using private-public key pair include that they are not user-friendly and if you lose the private key then there is no way to recover it. So, it adds a new responsibility for the users to secure their private key. The address of a user account acts as the account identifier on blockchain. The address of a user account is derived from the public key.

What are UTXOs?

Some blockchain applications use the UTXO model for transactions. Blockchain applications such as Bitcoin and MultiChain use this model. Even DLTs such as R3 Corda also use this model. Let's understand this model by understanding how Bitcoin transactions work.

In Bitcoin, a transactions is a collection of zero or more and outputs. These input and output objects are called **Unspent Transaction Outputs (UTXO)**. Outputs of transactions are used as inputs of future transactions. A UTXO can be used as input only once. Each UTXO in Bitcoin contains a denomination and an owner (a Bitcoin address). In this model, the balances of addresses in the unconsumed UTXOs are stored. For a transaction to be valid, these requirements should be met:

1. The transaction must contain a valid signature for the owner of each UTXO that it consumes
2. The total denomination of the UTXOs consumed must be equal to or greater than the total denomination of the UTXOs that it produces

A user's balance is computed as the total sum of the denominations of UTXOs that they own. A transaction can consume zero or more UTXOs and produce zero or more UTXOs. For a miner to pay reward to itself, it includes a transaction in the block that consumes zero UTXOs but produces one UTXO with the denomination assigned the amount of Bitcoin it is supposed to award itself.

A UTXO transaction model is suitable when blockchain transactions involve the transfer of asset, but for non-assets transfer transactions such as recording facts, invoking smart contracts, and so on, this model it not suitable.

Popular permissioned blockchain platforms

Now we have a basic idea about what a DApp, blockchain, and DLT is, let's have an overview of what platforms are available to build a permissioned blockchain applications and DApps. We will only go through the ones that are popular on the market, and for which there is a demand.

Ethereum

Ethereum is the most popular DApp after Bitcoin. Ethereum is a decentralized platform that allows us to build other blockchain-based DApps on top of it. In Ethereum, we build DApps using Ethereum smart contracts. Smart contracts are applications that run exactly as programmed without any possibility of downtime, censorship, fraud, or third-party interference. Ethereum can be thought of as a platform to deploy and run smart contracts. Ethereum supports two consensus protocols, PoW and PoA (Clique).

The main public Ethereum network uses PoW for consensus. If you want to deploy your own private Ethereum network, then you have to use PoA. PoW requires a lot of computation power to keep the blockchain secure, therefore it's good for public blockchain use, whereas PoA doesn't have any such computation power requirement; instead it requires a few authority nodes in the network to achieve consensus.

 You must be wondering why we need smart contracts to build DApps. Why cannot we simply put formatted messages on blockchain in the form of transactions and interpret them on client? Well, using smart contracts gives you both technical and business benefits.

Quorum

Quorum is a decentralized platform that allows us to build permissioned blockchain-based DApps on top of it. Actually, Quorum is a fork of Ethereum (actually Quorum is a fork of Go Ethereum, which is an implementation of Ethereum using Golang), therefore if you have ever worked on Ethereum then you will find it easy to learn and build permissioned blockchains using Quorum. Many enterprises select Quorum for building blockchains because of Ethereum's large community, which makes it easy to find Ethereum developers. What makes Quorum different from Ethereum is that it supports privacy (it lets parties do transactions privately); peer whitelisting, so you can mention a list of other nodes that are allowed to connect to your node (in Ethereum this needs to be done at network level); many different flavors of consensus protocols suitable for permissioned blockchain, and provides very high performance.

Quorum currently supports three consensus protocols, QuorumChain, IBFT, and Raft. We will skip QuorumChain in this book, as Raft and IBFT fulfil all our requirements.

Microsoft Azure provides BaaS to easily build your own Quorum network on the Cloud. But, in this book, we will learn how to install it manually, and we won't be using BaaS.

Parity

Popular node software for Ethereum include Go Ethereum, Ethereum C++, and Parity. Parity also supports two other consensus protocols, other than Ethereum's PoW, which are specifically designed for permissioned blockchains. These consensus protocols are Aura and Tendermint. Many Ethereum developers use parity compared to Quorum when they don't need the extra features provided by Quorum.

As parity doesn't provide any unique features compared to Quorum, we will be skipping parity in this book. But, once you finish this book, you will find it really easy to grasp parity's concepts and will be able to build something using it too.

MultiChain

MultiChain is a platform to build permissioned blockchain-based DApps. Unique features of MultiChain include permissions management, data streams, and assets. It doesn't support smart contracts. This is an example of a non-smart contract-based platform for building blockchain-based DApps. MultiChain uses round robin validation consensus.

Initially MultiChain was based on the idea of managing ownership and transfer of assets on blockchain. Operations on assets includes issuance, reissuance, transfer, atomic exchange, escrow, and destruction of assets. Later on, data streams were introduced to provide a different flavor of representing data in MultiChain. Any number of streams can be created in a MultiChain, and each stream acts as an independent append-only collection of items. Operations on streams include creating streams, writing, subscribing, indexing, and retrieving. So, basically, a blockchain use case on MultiChain can be built on a foundation of assets or streams. Finally, permission management is used to control who can connect, transact, create assets/streams, mine/validate, and administrate.

MultiChain provides maximal compatibility with the Bitcoin ecosystem, including the peer-to-peer protocol, transaction/block formats, the UTXO model, and Bitcoin Core APIs/runtime parameters. So, before you start learning MultiChain, it's better to learn how Bitcoin works at a high level at least.

Hyperledger Fabric 1.0

Before we get into what Hyperledger Fabric 1.0 is, we need to understand what Hyperledger is specifically. Hyperledger is an umbrella project of open source blockchains and related tools, started in December 2015 by the Linux Foundation. At the time of writing this book, there are four projects under Hyperledger:Fabric, Sawtooth, Iroha, and Burrow.

Hyperledger Fabric is the most popular project under Hyperledger. IBM is the main contributer to the project. IBM's Bluemix also provides BaaS to build your own Fabric network on the Cloud easily.

Hyperledger Fabric 1.0 is a platform to build your own permissioned blockchain-based applications. Currently, at the time of writing this book, Hyperledger Fabric 1.0 supports only distributed architecture, and for the creation of blocks it depends on a central trusted node called the **orderer**. It supports smart contracts, network permissioning, privacy, and other features. In HLF 1.0, there is a special kind of node called as **OSN**, which is hosted by a trusted party. This OSN creates blocks and distributes to peers in networks. As you trust this node, there is no need for consensus. HLD 1.0 currently supports CouchDB and LevelDB to store the state of the blockchain. Peers in the network store the state of the blockchain in the LevelDB database, by default.

HLF 1.0 has a concept of channels to achieve privacy. A channel is a sub-blockchain in the network and allows certain parties to be part of a channel depending on configuration. Actually, every transaction has to belong to a channel and when the HLF 1.0 network is deployed, a default channel is created. OSN can see all the data in all the channels, therefore it should a trusted party. Technically, it's possible to configure the network to have multiple OSNs hosting different channels if you cannot trust a single party for all channels. Even if the traffic is going to be huge or OSN availability is critical, then you can plug Kafka into OSN for better performance and increased stability. We can even have multiple OSNs per channel connected via Kafka if high availability is required.

Fabric 1.0 has a feature called **transaction endorsement**, which provides a mechanism of taking approvals from certain parties before sending a transaction. When we say that a transaction has been endorsed by a member in the network, we mean that the member has verified the transaction. Every chaincode (smart contracts in HLF) has an endorsement policy defined to it at the time of deployment. The policy states which members has to endorse the transactions associated with this chaincode. The default policy states that any one member of the channel has to sign the transaction. But, we can define custom policies containing **AND** and **OR** operators.

Also, peers of the same channel broadcast blocks to each other regardless of the presence or absence of OSN, but in the absence of OSN new blocks cannot be created for the channel. Peers broadcast blocks using a special protocol called as **gossip data dissemination protocol**.

HLF 1.0 has very advanced membership features to control network membership, and that are also internal to a specific organization. In HLF 1.0, you can write chaincodes in Java or Go programming languages. In the future, Fabric 1.0 will come with the **Simple Byzantine Fault Tolerance (SBFT)** consensus protocol and some other features that will enable us to build DApps. Similarly, there are various new features that are under development and will be released in future as a sub-version of the product.

The best way to get started with building your first HLF 1.0 application is the check out examples at https://github.com/hyperledger/fabric-samples and modify them according to your application needs. You can find HLF 1.0 detailed docs at http://hyperledger-fabric.readthedocs.io/en/latest/.

BigchainDB

BigchainDB is a decentralized database that uses blockchain. BigchainDB is highly scalable and customizable. It uses the Blockchain data structure. It supports features such as rich permissioning, petabytes capacity, advanced querying, linear scaling, and so on. At the time of writing this book, BigchainDB is not production-ready but can be used for building **Proof of Concepts (PoCs)**. We will learn how it works, and will create a basic PoC using it, in later chapters.

InterPlanetary File System

InterPlanetary File System (IPFS) is a decentralized filesystem. IPFS uses **Distributed Hash Table (DHT)** and Merkle **Direct Acyclic Graph (DAG)** data structures. It uses a protocol similar to Torrent to decide how to move the data around the network. One of the advanced features of IPFS is that it supports file versioning. To achieve file versioning, it uses data structures similar to Git.

Although it's called as a decentralized filesystem, it doesn't adhere to a major property of a filesystem, namely, when we store something in filesystem, it should be there until deleted. But, IPFS doesn't work this way. Each node doesn't store all files, instead it stores only those files it needs. Therefore, if a file is not popular, then many nodes will not have the file therefore there is a huge chance of the file disappearing in the network. Due to this, we can call IPFS a decentralised peer-to-peer file-sharing application. We will learn about about how it works in later chapters.

Corda

Corda is a platform on which to build your own permissioned DLT-based applications. Corda is a product of R3. R3 is an enterprise software firm working with over 100 banks, financial institutions, regulators, trade associations, professional services firms, and technology companies to develop Corda. The latest version of Corda is 1.0, which aims to replace legacy softwares used for financial transactions, and enables organisations to digitalize various business process that were cumbersome using legacy software systems:

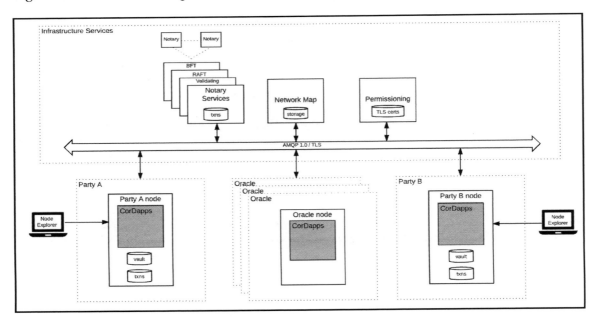

The preceding diagram shows the high level architecture of a Corda network. Let's understand Corda's architecture at a high level. The idea of R3's Corda is to provide a shared trusted ledger for financial transactions. R3's Corda is not a blockchain platform, therefore there is no concept of blocks, global broadcasts, and so on. All the transactions are point to point. Corda applications are not decentralized. In Corda, smart contracts are called as **CorDapps** and they are written in either Java or Kotlin.

Infrastructure services form the nodes in the network that should be hosted by the trusted parties. Network Map publishes IP addresses of all the other nodes, so that nodes can reach out to other nodes. Permissioning service gives permission to nodes to join the network ; the node will receive a root-authority-signed TLS certificate from the network's permissioning service if permitted to join the network. Notaries provide transaction ordering and time stamping services (optionally, a notary also acts as the timestamping authority, verifying that a transaction occurred during a specific time-window before notarizing it). A notary service may be a single network node, a cluster of mutually-trusting nodes, or a cluster of mutually-distrusting nodes.

Notaries are expected to be hosted by enterprises that the network doesn't trust, therefore consensus is required between the notaries, due to which Corda provides various pluggable consensus protocols, such as Raft, BFT, and so on.

Sometimes, Corda applications need to depend on external application APIs. For example, a multi-currency bank-to-bank payment application built using Corda will need to fetch the exchange rate. In this scenario, the node initiating the transaction can fetch the exchange rate and put on the transaction, but how can you trust that node? Also, every node cannot simply re-fetch the exchange rate to verify if it's correct because by the time other nodes fetch it the rate might have changed, and also this is not a scalable solution. Therefore, Corda provides oracles to solve this issue. There can be one or more oracles in the network. An Oracle is a service that acts as a bridge for communication between two applications. In Corda, the transaction initiator can fetch the information from outside the Corda network and get the information signed from **Oraclize** to prove its validity. Optionally, Oraclize can also provide the information to the transaction initiator on request. Obviously, the Oraclize should be hosted by trusted parties with respect to what information they provide and sign.

Corda supports any pluggable RDBMS (currently, it is using the H2 database) to store smart contracts data. Data privacy is maintained as to which nodes can see the transactions. Multisignature support is also given by the framework, which enables multiple nodes to sign a transaction. One of the major downsides of Corda is that as there is no global broadcasting, each node has to maintain its own backup and failover redundancy in a traditional way as there is no redundancy built into the network. A node will store transactions and retry sending the messages to the recipient until the recipient has successfully received it. Once the messages are received, the sender has no more responsibility.

Transaction validity

As all transactions are not broadcasted to all parties in the network, to prevent a double spend (a double spend is an attack on DLTs to spend the same money twice, transfer the same asset twice and so on), we use notaries. Notaries contain all the unconsumed UTXOs, and after notarization they mark them as consumed and add the new unconsumed ones to their state. The transaction purposer gets the transaction notarized by a notary before sending to the other parties for commit.

A notary will only be able to sign a transaction if it has earlier signed input states of the transaction. But, this may not always be the case, therefore Corda also lets us change the state's appointed notary. This situation can occur mostly due to the following reasons:

- A transaction consuming states that have different appointed notaries
- A node wishes to use a different notary for achieving privacy or efficiency

Before these transactions can be created, the states must first be repointed to all have the same notary. This is achieved using a special notary-change transaction.

CorDapps are not like smart contracts of other platforms. They don't have a state. Their purpose is to just validate if the outputs produced from the inputs are correct. Every UTXO points to a CorDapp. CorDapps define the format of UTXOs. In a transaction, we can have UTXOs of multiple CorDapps, and in these cases each CorDapp will run only once and validate all the inputs and outputs belonging to it. For a transaction to be valid, it must be contractually valid; the CorDapp should approve it.

Apart from inputs and outputs, transactions might consist of commands too, small data packets that the platform doesn't decipher itself but which help CorDapps to process the inputs and outputs. A command is a piece of data associated with some public keys. Commands are used to provide additional information to the CorDapps that it cannot get via the UTXOs. The platform assures that the transaction is signed by every key listed in the commands before the contracts start to execute. Thus, the CorDapp can trust that all listed keys have signed the transaction, but is responsible for verifying that the intended parties have signed it. Public keys may be random or identityless for privacy, or linked to a well-known legal identity.

Oracles provide signed information to the transaction purposer in the form of commands that encapsulate a specific fact, and list the oracle as a required signer.

Also, transactions can contain a hash of attachments. Attachments are ZIP/JAR files. Attachments are useful when there's a large fragment of data that can be reused across several different transactions.

It is possible that while verifying a proposed transaction, the node may not have all the transactions of the transaction chain that it needs to verify. Therefore, Corda lets the node request the missing transactions from the proposer(s). It's always true that the transaction proposer will have all the transactions of the required transaction chain, as they would have requested it when verifying the transaction and created the purposed transaction's input states.

Finally, once the transaction is committed, you can query the Vault (which keeps track of both unconsumed and consumed states).

> To learn more about Corda and build your first Corda app, visit `https://docs.corda.net/`, which contains detailed documentation. There are several example apps that you can download and experiment with.

Hyperledger Sawtooth

Sawtooth is a decentralized platform to build your own permissioned DApps. The main contributer to Sawtooth is Intel. What makes Sawtooth special is that it uses a **Trusted Execution Environment (TEE)** (it currently supports Intel's SGX only) for consensus, which makes the network very safe and trustworthy and increases trust in the final result of the consensus.

The TEE is a secure area of the main processor. It guarantees that the code and data loaded inside is protected with respect to confidentiality and integrity. The TEE as an isolated execution environment that provides security features such as isolated execution, integrity of Trusted Applications, along with confidentiality of their assets.

Proof of Elapsed Time (PoET) is the name of the consensus protocol that Sawtooth uses. In PoET, there are special types of nodes called as validators. Validators must run their node on an SGX-supported CPU. This is how PoET works.

Every validator requests a wait time from an enclave (a trusted function). The validator with the shortest wait time for a particular transaction block is elected the leader. One function, say `CreateTimer`, creates a timer for a transaction block that is guaranteed to have been created by the enclave. Another function, say `CheckTimer`, verifies that the timer was created by the enclave and, if it has expired, creates an attestation that can be used to verify that the validator did, in fact, wait the allotted time before claiming the leadership role. PoET randomly distributes leadership election across the entire population of validators. The probability of election is proportional to the resources contributed (in this case, resources are general-purpose processors with a TEE). An attestation of execution provides information for verifying that the certificate was created within the enclave (and that the validator waited the allotted time). Further, the low cost of participation increases the likelihood that the population of validators will be large, increasing the robustness of the consensus algorithm.

Sawtooth also supports smart contracts (specifically, Ethereum smart contracts can be executed on Sawtooth). Performance-wise, Sawtooth scales well in terms of large numbers of transactions and nodes.

Popular blockchain use cases

Let's see some of the popular use cases for permissioned blockchains. It will help us to understand what enterprises can use permissioned blockchains for and what use cases are valid for permissioned blockchains.

Everledger

Everledger is a digital registry for diamonds powered by blockchain. It's an example of supply chain management on blockchain. Blockchain was used because, in blockchain, records are immutable. Everledger uses more than 40 features, including color and clarity, to create a diamond's ID. When this information is placed on blockchain, this information becomes a certificate chronicling the jewel's ownership, from mine to ring. Everledger has digitized more than a million diamonds and partnered with firms including Barclays. Participants in the blockchain network, such as merchants, banks, and insurers, can verify if a diamond is legitimate. Everledger is built on the Hyperledger Fabric platform. In the future, they are also planning to add other precious goods to their blockchain.

Let's take an example scenerio and see how blockchain helps in this use case. Alice purchases a diamond, insures it, and registers it on the Everledger blockchain. Next, she loses the diamond and reports it as stolen. The insurance company then compensates her for the loss. Finally, Bob the thief attempts to sell the stolen diamond to Eve the jeweller. She requests verification from Everledger and finds out that it's a stolen diamond. The insurance company is notified about the stolen diamond and they take possession of it.

Walmart's food tracking

Walmart's food tracking use case is a combination of blockchain and IoT to make a food product's history transparent and traceable to it's origin. It's an example of supply chain management on blockchain. Walmart's food tracking supply chain management is built on top of the Hyperledger Fabric platform.

A lot of people die every year due to food poisoning. As soon as someone falls sick or dies due to food poisoning the authorities try to track the source of the food and make sure that all the food items from the source that are distributed is suspended from selling and is called back. This saves lives of a lot of people. But the issue is that as every participation in the supply chain have their own ways and processes storing and retrieving information therefore it takes weeks for the authorities to track the source prevent everyone in the chain from selling the food items. Blockchain in combination with the IoT might just be able to solve this problem.

With every party in the supply chain storing and retrieving information, blockchain can fasten the process of finding the source of a food item. The following list shows additional benefits blockchain can add:

- Consumers can see exactly where a food product was harvested.
- Due to panic over food poisoning, people tend to throw away clean food, which increases the amount of food wasted. Blockchain can pinpoint the tainted food, therefore preventing food waste.
- Each step in the supply chain is visible to everybody. Fraudulent food entering the market can be avoided.
- Blockchain can act as evidence that a tainted food items was shipped from a particular producer. Due to this, producers will take care and adhere to safe practices because, if they don't, they will be caught with the evidence.
- Finally every food item gets a story associated with it. This enables users to learn about the food item's history.

IoT technology, such as sensors and RFID tags, enables real-time data to be written on the blockchain as food products pass along the supply chain.

Let's see an example of what the blockchain records in this case, and who the participants are. The participants are farms from where the food originates, factories where they are packed and processed, cargo companies who ship the food, Walmart stores, and so on. The data recorded on the blockchain is farm origin data, the batch number, factory and processing data, expiration dates, storage temperatures, and shipping details.

Ghana's land registry

BenBen is a team of research and development engineers dedicated to building innovative products to improve government technology in Ghana. They developed a digital land registry solution using blockchain for Ghana citizens.

In Ghana, banks don't accept land as a collateral when giving loans. That's because in Ghana, a paper registry system is unenforceable in court. This is preventing millions of people from getting loans.

BenBen provides a top-of-stack land registry and verification platform for financial institutions. This platform captures transactions and verifies the data. BenBen works with financial institutions to update current registries, enable smart transactions, and distribute private keys for clients, to allow automated and trusted property transactions between all parties.

Dubai's housing rental

Dubai's housing rental use case is a blockchain application that let's individual expats lease an apartment or renew their housing tenancy contract online within minutes. In Dubai, if an individual wants to take an apartment for rent, then they have to provide KYC documents, cheques as a contract-term guarantee, and create an Ejari (a government contract to legalize the otherwise unpleasant relationship between landlords and tenants in Dubai). In Dubai, most real estate companies rent apartments only if you want to stay for a longer period of time (for instance, at least a year) and to make sure you obey the contract, they ask you to provide postdated cheques as a guarantee, as in Dubai, a cheque bounce is considered a criminal offence. As the process of renting an apartment and renewing the tenancy contract is a cumbersome process for both tenants and real estate companies, **Dubai Smart Government (DSG)** (a technology arm of Smart Dubai, a city-wide initiative to transform Dubai technologically) launched a mission to make this whole process easier and quicker using blockchain.

This housing rental application was built using Hyperledger Fabric 1.0, and initially seven entities participated in the network. DSG, **General Directorate of Residency and Foreigners Affairs Dubai (DNRD)**, wasl, **Dubai Land Department**, The **Dubai Electricity and Water Authority (DEWA)**, Emirates **National Bank of Dubai (NBD)**, and **Emirates Islamic (EI)** bank were the entities who shared their data on blockchain to make the tenancy contract creation and renewing easier.

Earlier, DSG and the **Emirates Identity Authority (EIDA)** launched DubaiID, which allowed Dubai residents a unified access to all eServices provided by government agencies through one login, and interaction with them via the internet. In this blockchain use case, the tenant had to log in to the real estate's portal using DubaiID; in this case, wasl's tenant must have a DubaiID to login. Once logged in, SDG will write the Emirates ID number into blockchain, and DNRD shares visa and passport information on the blockchain for that tenant. Then, wasl's portal redirects users to submit digital cheques using an Emirates NBD or EI bank account. Once digital cheques are submitted, a request is made to DLD via blockchain to renew or create an Ejari. Finally, once Ejari processing is done, DEWA is notified to activate the water and electricity supply. So basically, the first pilot was for individuals who wanted to lease or renew a wasl apartment and had a bank account with Emirates NBD or EI. Soon, more banks and real estate companies will be added to the network to provide this service for more people in Dubai. In this process, it was ensured that a piece of information can only be seen by the concerned parties.

This use case fits in well as a blockchain use case because a signed immutable ledger was required to store KYC, cheques, and Ejaris and the latter can be proved if the customer or any entity tries to commit fraud. For example, when Emirates NBD issues cheques, if they do it without blockchain and simply make point-to-point API calls, then there is a very good possibility of intentional and unintentional disagreement between ENBD, the tenant, and wasl regarding the existence of a digital cheque or its current status. Therefore, blockchain can be the final tool for reference if any dispute occurs.

Project Ubin

Project Ubin is a digital cash-on-ledger project run in partnership between **Monetary Authority of Singapore (MAS)** and R3, with the participation of **Bank of America (BOA) Merrill Lynch**, **Credit Suisse**, DBS bank, **The Hongkong and Shanghai Banking Corporation Limited**, J.P. Morgan, **Mitsubishi UFJ Financial Groupb (MUFG)**, OCBC bank, **Singapore Exchange (SGX)**, and **United Overseas Bank (UOB)**, as well as **BCS Information Systems** as a technology provider.

The aim of Project Ubin is building a digitalized form of the SGD (Singapore's national currency) on a distributed ledger to bring many benefits to Singapore's financial ecosystem. The benefits would be the same as that of any other cryptocurrencies.

Currently, this application is built using Quorum, but in future it may move to Corda as R3 is one of the partners.

MAS is Singapore's central bank and financial regulatory authority. MAS acts as a settlement agent, operator, and overseer of payment, clearing, and settlement systems in Singapore that focus on safety and efficiency.

Summary

In this chapter, we learned what DApps are and got an overview of blockchain-based DApps. We saw what a blockchain is, what its benefits are, and saw various platforms that we can use to build our own blockchain-based DApps. Finally, we saw some use cases and how blockchain can bring change to the financial and non-financial industry. In the next chapter, we will get into Ethereum and Quorum, and build a basic example DApp.

Building Blockchain Using 2 Quorum

In the previous chapter, we saw what a DApp, DLT, and blockchain are. We also saw an overview of some popular blockchain-based DApps. At present, Ethereum is the most popular public DApp after Bitcoin. In this chapter, we will learn how to build permissioned blockchain-based DApps using Quorum. We will learn about Quorum in depth by exploring all the various consensus protocols it supports, its permissioning and privacy features, and finally, tools that enable us to quickly deploy a Quorum network.

In this chapter, we will cover the following topics:

- User accounts in Ethereum
- What is a Merkle tree and what is it used for in blockchain?
- How do **Istanbul Byzantine Fault Tolerant (IBFT)** and Raft work?
- Various mechanisms supported by Quorum to achieve privacy
- Setting up constellation, Raft, and IBFT networks
- Various third-party tools or libraries related to Quorum

Overview of Quorum

Quorum is a permissioned decentralized platform that allows us to deploy DApps on top of it. DApps are created using one or more smart contracts. Smart contracts are programs that run exactly as programmed without any possibility of downtime, censorship, fraud, or third-party interface. In Quorum, smart contracts can be written in Solidity, LLL, or Serpent. Solidity is the preferred one. There can be multiple instances of a smart contract. Each instance is identified by a unique address, and you can deploy multiple DApps on the same Quorum network.

In Ethereum, there is an internal currency called **ether**. To deploy or execute smart contracts, you need to pay ether to the miners and as Quorum is a fork of Ethereum, the same thing exists here too. But in Quorum, ether is valueless and a fixed number of ether is generated at the **genesis block**, and no more ether can be generated after that. Both user accounts and smart contracts can hold ether. In Quorum, you need to have some ether to execute transactions on the network, but ether is not deducted and sending ether to another account doesn't deduct ether, therefore you can say ether in Quorum provides a way to track the owner of a account if anything suspicious is by a account by tracking the ether transfers and also provide a way such that to make transactions you need to get permission from one of the permitted members; that is, get some ether from a network member.

Currently, Quorum supports three consensus protocols: QuorumChain, IBFT, and Raft. In this book, we will learn only about Raft and IBFT as they are the most-used ones. For privacy, it supports two mechanisms: the zero-knowledge security layer protocol and private contracts. We will learn about private contracts but will not be covering ZSL as it's still not production-ready.

Ethereum accounts

To create an account, we just need an asymmetric key pair. There are various algorithms, such as **Rivest–Shamir–Adleman (RSA)** and **Elliptic Curve Cryptography (ECC)** for generating asymmetric key pairs. Ethereum uses ECC. ECC has various curves. These curves have a different speed and security. Ethereum uses **secp256k1** curves. To go in to ECC and it's curves will require mathematical knowledge, and it's not necessary to understand it in depth to build DApps using Ethereum.

Ethereum uses 256-bit encryption. An Ethereum private and public key is a 256-bit number. As processors cannot represent such big numbers therefore it's always encoded as a hexadecimal string of length 64.

Every account is represented by an address. Once we have the keys we need to generate the address, here is the procedure to generate the address, and here is the procedure to generate the address from the public key:

1. First, generate the **Keccak-256** hash of the public key. It will give you a 256-bit number.
2. Drop the first 90 bits and 12 bytes. You should now have 160 bits of binary data (20 bytes).
3. Now, encode the address as a hexadecimal string. So, finally, you will have a byte string of 40 characters, which is your account address.

Now, anyone can send ether to this address, and then you can sign and send transactions from this address.

What are Ethereum transactions?

A transaction is a data package to transfer ether from an account to another account or contract, invoke methods of a contract, or deploy a new contract. A transaction is using **Elliptic Curve Digital Signature Algorithm (ECDSA)**, which is a digital signature algorithm based on ECC. A transaction contains a signature identifying the sender and proving their intention, the amount of ether to transfer, the maximum number of computational steps the transaction execution is allowed to take (called a **gas limit**), and the cost the sender of the transaction is willing to pay for each computational step (called the **gas price**). The product of the gas used and the gas price is called the **transaction fees**.

In permissioned networks, ether is valueless. In a Quorum network, ether is supplied in the genesis block and is not generated dynamically at runtime. You need to supply ether in the genesis block. You need to provide gas to prevent attacks, such as infinite loops. Ether is not deducted from accounts when transactions are mined.

If the transaction's intention is to invoke a method of a contract, it also contains input data, or if its intention is to deploy a contract, then it can contain the initialization code. To send ether or to execute a contract method, you need to broadcast a transaction to the network. The sender needs to sign the transaction with its private key.

A transaction is said to be confirmed if we are sure that it will always appear in the blockchain at the same place. In Ethereum's proof of work, it's recommended to wait for the transaction to appear 15 blocks below the newest block (that is, wait for 15 confirmations) before assuming the transaction to be confirmed as there are chances of forking and the transaction disappearing from the blockchain. But, in Quorum's Raft or IBFT, as soon as the transaction appears in one of the blocks, we can say it's confirmed as there is no possibility of forking.

What is a Merkle tree?

Before we get into what a Merkle root in blocks of blockchain is, let's understand the structure of blockchain. A block is made up of two parts; the first part is the block header and the second part is the set of transactions of that block. The block header contains information such as the previous block hash (it's actually a hash of the previous block's header), timestamp, Merkle root, and information related to achieving consensus.

At the time of sync, while downloading a block a node downloads the block header and the block's transactions. Now, how would the receiving node know that these transactions are actually part of that block and are in the correct order? Every block is identified by a unique hash, but the block hash is not part of the block header and is uniquely calculated by every node after downloading the block; therefore we cannot use the idea of a block hash. Instead, we can rely on something like a transactions hash; a hash stored in the block header, which is calculated by combining all transactions and hashing it. This idea will work perfectly, and we can detect if any transaction is missing or extra transactions included, or if transactions are in the correct order.

Well, a Merkle root is an alternative to the transactions hash approach but provides another major advantage: it allows the network to have light nodes. We can, of course, have blockchain implemented without Merkle root, but if there is a need for light nodes in the network, then Merkle roots are required to be used. A light node is one that only downloads block headers but no transactions but still it should be able to provide all APIs to the client. For example: a smartphone cannot have the full blockchain as it could be very large in size; therefore, we can install a light client in smartphones.

Let's first understand what a binary Merkle tree is with respect to blockchain. A hash tree or Merkle tree is a tree in which every leaf node is a hash of a transaction, and every non-leaf node is a hash of the hashes of its child nodes. Hash trees allow efficient and secure verification of which transactions are part of the block. Every blocks forms it's own Merkle tree. A Merkle tree is called a **binary Merkle tree** when every parent has two children. Binary Merkle trees are what is used in blockchain. Here is an example of a binary Merkle tree:

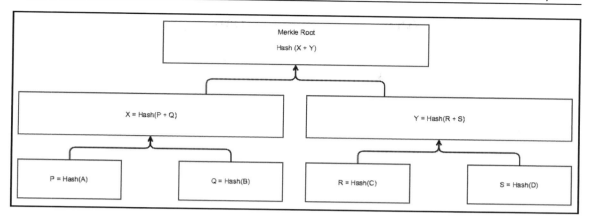

In the preceding diagram, at first the individual hash of every transaction is calculated. Then, they are grouped into two. And then, a hash of the two hashes is calculated for each pair. This process will continue until we have a single hash called the **Merkle root**. In case there are odd numbers of transactions, the last transaction is duplicated to make the total number of transactions even.

Now, at the time of downloading a complete block, the block header, and transactions of the block, a node can verify whether the set of transactions is correct or not by forming the binary Merkle tree and checking that the generated Merkle root is the same as the one included in the block header. Of course, this can be done without a Merkle tree, as discussed previously.

A light node can take advantage of the Merkle tree to serve requests to the client. For example, a light node can make a request to a full node asking if a particular transaction is committed in a block or not, and the full node replies with the block number and Merkle proof if the transaction is committed in a block. A light node cannot just believe the full node if the full node provides a block number, therefore the full node also provides Merkle proof. To understand what a Merkle proof is, let's take the preceding diagram and a scenario where the light node asks the full node if TxD is committed or not. Now, the full node returns the block number along with a sub-tree, which is H_{ABCD}, H_{AB}, H_{CD}, H_C, and H_D. This sub-tree is the Merkle proof. Now, the light client can take this Merkle proof and verify it. Verification will include looking at whether the Merkle proof is constructed correctly and whether the Merkle root of the Merkle proof is the same as the Merkle root present in the block header of the block that the full node claimed the transaction was in. You must be wondering, what if a full node claims that the transaction is not committed even after it's committed? In this case, the only way to tackle this issue is to request multiple full nodes, and it's unlikely all of them will lie. This functionality cannot be achieved without Merkle trees.

Ethereum blockchain is more complicated. Now, suppose an Ethereum light node wants to know the balance of an account, read data from a smart contract, find the gas estimation for a transaction, and so on, then with this simple transactions binary Merkle will not be able to provide this functionality. So, in Ethereum, every block header contains not just one Merkle tree, but three trees for three kinds of objects:

- Transactions
- Transaction receipts (essentially, pieces of data showing the effect of each transaction)
- State

As we now have three trees, let's take an advanced query example that a light node would make to a full node. The query is *pretend to run this transaction on this contract. What would the transaction receipt and new state be?* This is handled by the state tree, but the way that it is computed is more complex. Here, we need to construct what can be a **Merkle state** transition proof. Essentially, it is a proof that makes the claim: if you run transaction T on the state with root S, the result will be a state with root S', with transaction receipt R. To compute the state transaction proof, the full node locally creates a fake block, sets the state to S, and pretends to be a light node while applying the transaction. That is, if the process of applying the transaction requires the light node to determine the balance of an account, the light node makes a balance query. If the light node needs to check a particular item in the storage of a particular contract, the light node makes a query for that, and so on. The full node *responds* to all of its own queries correctly, but keeps track of all the data that it sends back. The full node then sends the light node the combined data from all of these requests as a proof. The light client then undertakes the exact same procedure, but using the provided proof as its database instead of making requests to the full node and if its result is the same as what the full node claims, the light client accepts output to be the one full node claims to be.

 For state, Ethereum uses the Merkle Patricia tree instead of the binary tree. For the state tree, the situation is more complex. The state in Ethereum essentially consists of a key-value map, where the keys are addresses and the values are account balance, nonce, code, and storage for each account (where the storage is itself a tree). To learn how the Merkle Patricia tree works, visit https://easythereentropy.wordpress.com/2014/06/04/ understanding-the-ethereum-trie/.

In enterprise blockchains, there is no use of light clients as the nodes represent an enterprise, and enterprises have infrastructure to run full nodes.

What is forking in blockchain?

A fork is said to have happened when there is a conflict among the nodes regarding the validity of the blockchain, that is, more than one blockchain happens to be in the network. There are three kinds of fork: regular, soft, and hard.

A regular fork is said to be happening when there are two or more blocks at the same height. It is a temporary conflict and is resolved automatically. This is resolved by nodes by selecting the most accurate blockchain. For example, in proof-of-work, if two miners mine a block at the same time then it creates a regular fork. And, this is resolved by selecting the blockchain with the highest difficulty as the most accurate one.

A soft fork, by contrast, is any change to the blockchain protocol that's backward-compatible. Say, instead of 2 MB blocks, a new rule might only allow 1 MB blocks. Non-upgraded nodes will still see the new transactions as valid (1 MB is less than 2 MB in this example). However, if non-upgraded nodes continue to create blocks, the blocks they create will be rejected by the upgraded nodes. So, if the minority of a nodes in the network are upgraded then the chain they will form will become less accurate and overridden by the blockchain created by the non-upgraded nodes. Soft forks are resolved when the majority of the nodes in the network upgrade their node software.

A hard is a software upgrade that introduces a new rule to the network that isn't with the older software. You can think of a hard fork as an expansion of the rules. For example, a new rule that allows the block size to be 2 MB instead of 1 MB would require a hard fork. Nodes that continue running the old version of the software will see new transactions as invalid. So, the fork can only be resolved when all the nodes in the network upgrade their node software. Until then, there will be two different blockchains in the network.

 You must have heard about Bitcoin and Ethereum forks. For example, Bitcoin cash and Ethereum classic were formations of hard forks. Many miners and nodes in the network didn't agree to the new protocol and chose to run the old software, and split out of the network and formed a different network.

Raft consensus

Let's see how the Raft consensus protocol works at a level which will make us comfortable enough to build DApps. We won't go in depth into Raft as it's not necessary.

Raft is used in a semi-trusted network, and there is a desire for faster blocktimes (on the order of milliseconds instead of seconds) and single confirmation (the absence of regular forks).

Every node in the network keeps a list of all other nodes in the network regardless of whether they are up and running or not. A server in a Raft cluster is either a leader or a follower, and can be a candidate in the case of an election, which happens when the leader is unavailable. There can be only one leader at a time. The leader is responsible for creating and sending blocks to the followers. It regularly informs the followers of its existence by sending a heartbeat message. Each follower has a timeout (typically between 150 and 300 ms) called the **election timeout**, in which it expects the heartbeat from the leader. Every node uses a randomized election timeout in the range of 120-300 ms. The election timeout is reset on receiving the heartbeat. If no heartbeat is received, the follower changes its status to candidate and starts the leader election to elect a new leader in the network. When a candidate starts the leader election, it basically purposes itself as the new leader and becomes the leader if more than 50% of nodes vote for it. If a leader is not elected in a certain timeout, then a new leader election process is started. It's not necessary to understand the leader election process in depth.

Raft is designed in such a way that a Raft network requires more than 50% of the nodes to be available for new transactions to get committed to the blockchain; if the cluster has $2 * F + 1$ nodes it can tolerate F failures and still function correctly. If more than F nodes fail, then the application will fail and it will again resume working properly once the cluster again has more than F nodes working properly. Even leader election will fail if more than 50% nodes are not available in the network.

Every transaction from every node is sent to every other node in the network. The leader is responsible for creating and broadcasting blocks. When a leader creates a block, it will first send the block to all the followers, and once more than 50% of the followers receive the block, the leader will commit the block to its blockchain and then send a commit message to the followers so that the followers also commit the block to their blockchain. In the case of unavailability of the followers, the leader retries the requests indefinitely until the block is eventually committed by all of the followers. This process makes sure that once a block is committed to blockchain, it can never be reversed. Even the leader election process makes sure that whoever is selected as a leader has its blockchain up to date.

In Quorum, the default block time is 50 ms, and you can change that according to your needs. So, every 50 ms, a block is created, but remember that if there are no transactions then blocks are not created; empty blocks are not created in Raft. The leader can create new blocks and send them to followers before the previous block is committed, and block creation is asynchronous. But of course, they are committed serially. When a node starts up, it retrieves the missed blocks from the leader only, not from other nodes in the network.

 For the Raft cluster to function properly, it's very important that the average time it takes a server to send a heartbeat request to every server in the cluster and receive responses is less than the election timeout. Also, there is no way for the leader to delete or modify committed blocks; a leader can only append new blocks to the blockchain.

Istanbul Byzantine Fault Tolerence

Let's see how the IBFT consensus protocol works at a level that will make us comfortable enough to build DApps. We won't go in depth into IBFT as it's not necessary.

IBFT is a type of proof-of-authority protocol. In IBFT, there are two kinds of nodes: validator nodes (referred to as authorities when they are linked to physical entities) and regular nodes. Authority nodes are the ones that create blocks. IBFT is used in a network where there is a need for BFT, blocktime up to a few seconds is good enough, and we need a single confirmation (the absence of regular forks).

The system can tolerate at most F Byzantium or crashed nodes in a N validator nodes network that is, $F = (N-1)/3$. The default block time in IBFT is between one to ten seconds and Quorum does allow you to customize this.

In IBFT, a round involves creating and committing a new block to the blockchain. A new round is started once a new block is committed in the $(2F + 1)$ validators blockchain. Before each block creation round, the validators will pick one of them as the proposer. The proposer is the validator responsible for creating the block. For the block to be committed to the blockchain, it must be signed by at least $(2F + 1)$ validators. So, there is a process which involves sending and receiving various messages between the purposer and other validators at each round to agree to the new block.

There are two algorithms supported by Quorum for selection of the purposer: round robin and sticky purposer. Round robin is used by default, and in round robin algorithms the purposer is selected in round robin fashion. But, in the sticky purposer algorithm, a single validator becomes the purposer for all rounds, and if the purposer crashes then the next validator is selected as the new purposer, which again remains the sole purposer for all rounds; the purposer remains constant until it fails. Regardless of the round robin or sticky purposer algorithm, if the purposer fails to commit a block in *1-10* seconds time, then a new round is started and the next validator becomes the purposer of the new round.

If the network manages to have more than *F* faulty nodes, then these faulty nodes can prevent creation of new blocks by declining to sign blocks. When a crashed node in the network comes up, it can get missed blocks from any node in the network. There is no way more than *F* faulty nodes can rewrite blocks.

The list of validators is stored in the header of genesis blocks, and the `extraData` field in the header contains the list of validators. For the first round, the first validator is selected. The header also contains various other fields and details related to IBFT to help the network reach consensus.

A validator can add or remove a validator. Even adding or removing new validators to the network requires *2F + 1* validators agreeing to it. This process of validators agreeing or disagreeing to adding or removing a validator is done manually. It cannot be an automatic process as validators can start adding multiple validating nodes of their own and compromise the network. Therefore, a manual process makes sure that other validators learn who the new validator is and decide whether to allow it or not.

 You can learn more about how IBFT works in depth at `https://github.com/ethereum/EIPs/issues/650`.

Private contracts and constellation

Private contracts are an out-of-the-box feature provided by Quorum for enabling data privacy. Private contracts are used for sharing information privately between two or more nodes without other nodes being able to see it.

Let's look at what private contracts in Quorum are. Contracts that are deployed using private transactions are called **private contracts**. A private transaction is basically one whose payload (contract code for contract deployment or function arguments for calling functions, the data part of transactions) is shared point to point, outside of blockchain between a selected list of peers mentioned at the time of sending the transaction, and the hash of the payload is recorded in the blockchain by replacing the actual payload with the hash of the payload. Now, the nodes in the network check whether they have the content that hashes to the hash present in the blockchain as payload, and if yes, then they execute the original payload. Quorum forms two different states of the same blockchain: the public and private state. Private transactions form the private state, whereas public transactions form the public state. These states cannot interact with each other. But, private-private contracts can certainly interact with each other.

Quorum uses constellation for sending and receiving actual transaction payloads for private transactions. Constellation is a separate software built by J.P. Morgan. Constellation forms a network of nodes, each of which advertises a list of public keys that they are the recipient for. Each node exposes an API which allows the user to send a payload to one or more public keys. That payload will be encrypted for the public key before being transferred over to the recipient node. It exposes APIs via IPC for applications to connect to their constellation node and send or receive data. At a high level, if you are connected to a constellation network, then you just have to mention the public key of the recipient and the data is encrypted and sent to the IP address mapped to the public key. While sending a private transaction, the list of public keys and the transaction is only broadcast to the blockchain network once the payload is successfully sent to all the listed constellation nodes. If any listed constellation node is down, then the transaction fails and is never broadcast to the blockchain network.

So, basically, before starting your Quorum node, you need to start your constellation node and then provide the IPC path for constellation to the Quorum node before starting the Quorum node. Then, your Quorum node uses the constellation for sending or receiving private transactions.

Private transactions are not the ultimate solution to achieving privacy in Quorum. They have various downsides. Following are some of them:

- Once you send a private transaction to a list of nodes, you cannot add new nodes to that list. For example, if you deployed a private contract that used for interbank transfers. Suppose initially the central bank was not part of the network, and later if they decide to join in then they won't be able to monitor the transactions because there is no way we can make the private contract visible to them nor the previous bank transfers visible to them. Although they can see the new private transactions, as they don't have the new private transactions they cannot execute the transactions and so will not be able to see the output.
- There is no way to check whether private transactions pointing to a private contracts have exactly the same list of public keys that were used while deploying the private contracts. This can lead to double spend attacks; in other words, you will be able to transfer the same assets twice. For example, it at the time of deploying contracts you mentioned three nodes *A*, *B*, and *C*. Now, when *A* is transferring assets it may exclude *C* from the private transaction and then later transfer the same assets to *C* by creating a new private transaction. There is no way for *C* to verify that the new owner of the asset is *B*. For this reason, private transactions aren't used for transferring digital assets, but private transactions can used for all other forms of data representation.
- You will need to build your own backup mechanisms for the constellation nodes. So, if your constellation node crashes, then it will not automatically get back payloads from the constellation network.

Installing Quorum and constellation

Now we are quite confident about the Quorum's consensus protocols, Ethereum accounts, transactions, and private contracts. It's time to build a Quorum network. Before that, we need to learn how to install Quorum and constellation. Remember that constellation is optional and should only be integrated in the Quorum network if private contracts are required.

The best way to install Quorum and constellation is to build the source code. In this book, we will concentrate on steps for Ubuntu and macOS only. You can find Quorum's source code at `https://github.com/jpmorganchase/quorum`, whereas you can find constellation source code at `https://github.com/jpmorganchase/constellation`.

Following are the three basic commands to build Quorum from source code:

```
git clone https://github.com/jpmorganchase/quorum.git
cd quorum
make all
```

Now, go into the `build/bin/` directory and you will find the `geth` executable, which is the node software for running the Quorum node. Also, you will find another executable file named `bootnode`, and we will use this to generate the enode ID only. We will see later what an enode ID is.

To install constellation, you need a few prerequisites. In Ubuntu, run the following commands to install the prerequisites:

```
apt-get install libdb-dev libleveldb-dev libsodium-dev zlib1g-dev libtinfo-dev
curl -sSL https://get.haskellstack.org/ | sh
stack setup
```

And, in macOS, run the following commands to install the prerequisites:

```
brew install berkeley-db leveldb libsodium
brew install haskell-stack
stack setup
```

Now, to install constellation, run the following commands:

```
git clone https://github.com/jpmorganchase/constellation.git
cd constellation
stack install
```

Now, after you run they preceding commands and they are executed successfully, you will get a message stating the path of the `constellation-node` executable. Move the executable from that path to a place where you can find it easily.

Build your first Raft network

Now, we have installed Quorum and constellation successfully, it's time to set up our first Quorum network. Before setting up the network, you need to decide whether you want to use Raft or IBFT, and accordingly you need to plan and set up. We will learn setting up both kinds of networks. We will also set up a constellation network.

Now, let's build a Raft network with constellation. We will also see how to add and remove new nodes once the network is up and running. We will build a network of four nodes.

Create a directory named `raft`. Then, place the `geth` and `constellation-node` binaries in it. You can use the `--help` option of `geth` and `constellation-node` to find the various sub-commands and options available.

Setting up a constellation network

Now, let's first create four constellation nodes. For development purposes, we will run all four nodes in the same machine. For every constellation node, we have to generate a separate asymmetric key pair. Run the following commands in the `raft` directory to create the key pairs:

```
./constellation-node --generatekeys=node1
./constellation-node --generatekeys=node2
./constellation-node --generatekeys=node3
./constellation-node --generatekeys=node4
```

Here, we are generating a single public key for each constellation node. But, you can have multiple public keys for each constellation node. At the time of running the preceding commands, it will ask you to enter a password to encrypt the keys, but you can skip that by pressing the *Enter* key. In case you want to encrypt at the time of running the constellation node, you have to provide the password for decryption. To keep things simple, we will not set a password.

While starting a constellation node, you need to pass the various required and optional variables, such as the URL to advertize to other nodes (reachable by them), the local port to listen on, the directory to store the payload, public keys, private keys, TLS settings, and so on. You can pass these variables to the constellation node as options to the command, or else in the form of a configuration file. Let's create a configuration file for each constellation node, which will provide these settings for the constellation nodes to start. Following are the configuration files for the constellation nodes:

Here is the code for `constellation1.conf`:

```
url = "http://127.0.0.1:9001/"
port = 9001
storage = "dir:./cnode_data/cnode1/"
socket = "./cnode_data/cnode1/constellation_node1.ipc"
othernodes = ["http://127.0.0.1:9002/", "http://127.0.0.1:9003/",
"http://127.0.0.1:9004/"]
publickeys = ["./cnode1.pub"]
privatekeys = ["./cnode1.key"]
tls = "off"
```

Here is the code for `constellation2.conf`:

```
url = "http://127.0.0.1:9002/"
port = 9002
storage = "dir:./cnode_data/cnode2/"
socket = "./cnode_data/cnode1/constellation_node2.ipc"
othernodes = ["http://127.0.0.1:9001/"]
publickeys = ["./cnode2.pub"]
privatekeys = ["./cnode2.key"]
tls = "off"
```

Here is the code for `constellation3.conf`:

```
url = "http://127.0.0.1:9003/"
port = 9003
storage = "dir:./cnode_data/cnode3/"
socket = "./cnode_data/cnode1/constellation_node3.ipc"
othernodes = ["http://127.0.0.1:9001/"]
publickeys = ["./cnode3.pub"]
privatekeys = ["./cnode3.key"]
tls = "off"
```

Here is the code for `constellation4.conf`:

```
url = "http://127.0.0.1:9004/"
port = 9004
storage = "dir:./cnode_data/cnode4/"
socket = "./cnode_data/cnode1/constellation_node4.ipc"
othernodes = ["http://127.0.0.1:9001/"]
publickeys = ["./cnode4.pub"]
privatekeys = ["./cnode4.key"]
tls = "off"
```

Here, the variable's name reveals what the variable is all about. One important thing to notice here is that we are not providing the other three nodes' URLs in the last three nodes, because constellation has a built-in auto-discovery protocol to find nodes in the network. So, here the first node is pointing to the last three, and the last three have a connection to the first, but in the end all will be able to find each other.

Now, run the following commands in different shell windows to start the constellation nodes:

```
./constellation-node constellation1.conf
./constellation-node constellation2.conf
./constellation-node constellation3.conf
./constellation-node constellation4.conf
```

Generating enodes

In Raft, before setting up the network you have to decide the total number of nodes that will be in the network, and then generate and enode ID for each. Then, you create a `static-nodes.json` file listing the enode URL of all the nodes, and feed this file to every node in the network. Adding nodes to the network once the network is set up involves a different process.

 Before going further, you need to know what an enode in Ethereum is. An enode is a way to describe an Ethereum node in the form of a URI. Every node in the network has a different enode. The enode conatins a 512-bit public key called a **node ID**, which is used to verify communication from a particular node on the network. The encode also contains the IP address and port number along with the node ID. The private key associated with the node ID is called a **node key**.

We will set up a network of three nodes, and then add the fourth node dynamically. Use the following three commands to generate the node keys of all four nodes:

```
./bootnode -genkey enode_id_1
./bootnode -genkey enode_id_2
./bootnode -genkey enode_id_3
./bootnode -genkey enode_id_4
```

The preceding command will create the private keys. Now, to find the node ID, you need to run the following commands:

```
./bootnode -nodekey enode_id_1
./bootnode -nodekey enode_id_2
./bootnode -nodekey enode_id_3
./bootnode -nodekey enode_id_4
```

The preceding commands will not create any new file; instead they will simply print a sample node URL with the actual node ID associated with the corresponding private key. For example: `enode://[nodeID]@[IP]:[port]`.

Now, create a `static-nodes.json` file and add the following code. Make sure you replace the node IDs with your generated ones:

```
[
"enode://480cd6ab5c7910af0e413e17135d494d9a6b74c9d67692b0611e4eefea1cd082ad
bdaa4c22467c583fb881e30fda415f0f84cfea7ddd7df45e1e7499ad3c680c@127.0.0.1:23
000?raftport=21000",
"enode://60998b26d4a1ecbb29eff66c428c73f02e2b8a2936c4bbb46581ef59b2678b7023
d300a31b899a7d82cae3cbb6f394de80d07820e0689b505c99920803d5029a@127.0.0.1:23
```

```
001?raftport=21001",
"enode://e03f30b25c1739d203dd85e2dcc0ad79d53fa776034074134ec2bf128e609a0521
f35ed341edd12e43e436f08620ea68d39c05f63281772b4cce15b21d27941e@127.0.0.1:23
002?raftport=21002"
]
```

Here, `2300x` ports are for Ethereum protocol communication, and `2100x` ports are for Raft protocol communication.

In Ethereum, `static-nodes.json` is used to list enodes of some nodes that you always want to connect to. And, using these nodes, your node can discover other nodes in the network. But, in the case of Quorum's Raft, this file has to include the enode of all the nodes in the network, as in Raft this file is used for achieving consensus, unlike in Ethereum, where this file is used for nodes discovery.

Creating an account

Now, we need to generate an Ethereum account. We are doing this now because at the time of creating the genesis block, we have to supply ether to the network. So, we will supply ether to this generated account. Here is the command for creating an Ethereum account:

```
./geth --datadir ./accounts account new
```

At the time of running this command, it will ask for a password to encrypt the account. You can press the *Enter* key twice and skip. This will make an empty string the password to decrypt the account. Here, the `--datadir` option is used to mention where to store the key. Basically, in the `accounts/keystore` directory, you will find a file with the format `UTC--DATE-TIME--ADDRESS`. Rename this file to `key1`. This file stores the private key and address of the account. Open the file and copy the address, as you will need it while creating the genesis block.

Creating the genesis block

Now, the last step is to create the genesis block. The genesis block is always hardcoded in the network. Here is the genesis block content. Create a `genesis.json` file and place the following code in it:

```
{
    "alloc": {
        "0x65d8c00633404140986e5e23aa9de8ea689c1d05": {
            "balance": "1000000000000000000000000000000"
```

```
        }
    },
    "coinbase": "0x0000000000000000000000000000000000000000",
    "config": {
        "homesteadBlock": 0
    },
    "difficulty": "0x0",
    "extraData": "0x",
    "gasLimit": "0x7FFFFFFFFFFFFFFF",
    "mixhash": "0x00000000000000000000000000000000
        647572616c65787365646c6578",
    "nonce": "0x0",
    "parentHash": "0x000000000000000000000000000000000
        000000000000000000000000000000000",
    "timestamp": "0x00"
}
```

Here, make sure you replace the account address,
`0x65d8c00633404140986e5e23aa9de8ea689c1d05`, with your account address. Here,
we supplied ether to the `0x65d8c00633404140986e5e23aa9de8ea689c1d05` account.

 If you want to get rid of ether in a Quorum network, you can use the `--gasPrice 0` option while starting `geth`. Therefore, you will not need to supply ether in the genesis block. But, ether gives the advantage of traceability.

Starting nodes

Now, before we start the nodes, we need to initialize them and create data directories for each node; copy the `static-nodes.json` file in each node's data directory, copy the account keys to the data directory, and Bootstrap the blockchain with the genesis block.

An Ethereum node's data directory structure includes `geth` and `keystore` directories, and also, a `static-nodes.json` file. The `keystore` directory contains accounts files and the `geth` directory contains all other data related to Ethereum, such as blockchain transactions, state, and the enode key.

Following are the commands to do all the initialize operations for all the nodes:

```
#Configuring Node 1
#'keystore' dir stores acccounts and 'geth' dir stores all other data
mkdir -p qdata/node1/{keystore,geth}
cp static-nodes.json qdata/node1
cp accounts/keystore/key1 qdata/node1/keystore
```

```
cp enode_id_1 qdata/node1/geth/nodekey
./geth --datadir qdata/node1 init genesis.json #bootstrap the blockchain

#Configuring Node 2
mkdir -p qdata/node2/geth
cp static-nodes.json qdata/node2
cp enode_id_2 qdata/node2/geth/nodekey
./geth --datadir qdata/node2 init genesis.json

#Configuring Node 3
mkdir -p qdata/node3/geth
cp static-nodes.json qdata/node3
cp enode_id_3 qdata/node3/geth/nodekey
./geth --datadir qdata/node3 init genesis.json
```

The preceding commands are self-explanatory. Now, run the following commands to start the Quorum nodes. Run each command in a new shell window:

```
#Starting node 1
PRIVATE_CONFIG=constellation1.conf ./geth --datadir qdata/node1 --port
23000 --raftport 21000 --raft --ipcpath "./geth.ipc"

#Starting node 2
PRIVATE_CONFIG=constellation2.conf ./geth --datadir qdata/node2 --port
23001 --raftport 21001 --raft --ipcpath "./geth.ipc"

#Starting node 3
PRIVATE_CONFIG=constellation3.conf ./geth --datadir qdata/node3 --port
23002 --raftport 21002 --raft --ipcpath "./geth.ipc"
```

Here is the meaning of the different options we provided:

- PRIVATE_CONFIG: This variable is used to make geth aware of the constellation node which it needs to send the private payload to. It points to the constellation node's configuration file.
- --datadir: Data directory to store state, transactions, accounts, and so on.
- --raft: This is used to specify that we want to run a Raft consensus.
- --port: The port to bind for the Ethereum transport.
- --raft-port: The port to bind for the Raft transport.
- --ipcpath: Filename for the IPC socket and pipe. IPC is enabled by default.

`geth` provides JSON-RPC APIs for clients to communicate with it. `geth` serves JSON-RPC APIs using HTTP, WS, and IPC. The APIs provided by JSON-RPC are divided into various categories. `geth` also provides an interactive JavaScript console to interact with it programatically using JavaScript APIs. The interactive console uses JSON-RPC over IPC to communicate with `geth`. We will learn more about this later.

Now, to open the interactive console of `node1`, use the following command:

```
./geth attach ipc:./qdata/node1/geth.ipc
```

Now, we have completed creating our first Raft network.

Adding or removing nodes dynamically

Now, let's add the fourth node dynamically. Any node can add the fourth node to the network. Let's add it from `node1`. The first step is to do the initialize operations for `node4`. Run the following commands for this:

```
#Configuring Node 4
mkdir -p qdata/node4/geth
cp enode_id_4 qdata/node4/geth/nodekey
./geth --datadir qdata/node4 init genesis.json
```

Note that, here, we didn't copy the `static-nodes.json` file, as we are adding it dynamically. Now, from the fourth node's interactive console, run the following line of code to add the fourth peer to the network:

```
raft.addPeer("enode://27d3105b2c1173792786ab40e466fda80edf9582cd7fa1a867123
dab9e2f170be0b7e16d4065cbe81637759555603cc0619fcdf0fc7296d506b9c26c26f3ae0c
@127.0.0.1:23003?raftport=21003")
```

Here, replace the node ID with your generated one. When you run the following command, you will get a number as a return value. This number is important, and is called the Raft ID of the node. Raft consensus assigns a unique ID to every node. The first node in the `static-nodes.json` file is given Raft if 1, the next one is given Raft ID 2, and so on. The fourth node will have Raft ID 4. While starting the fourth node you will need this number. Now, start the fourth node using the following command:

```
PRIVATE_CONFIG=constellation4.conf ./geth --datadir qdata/node4 --port
23003 --raftport 21003 --raft --ipcpath "./geth.ipc" --raftjoinexisting 4
```

In the preceding command, everything looks similar except a new option, `--raftjoinexisting`. While starting nodes that were added dynamically, we need to specify this option and assign it to the node's Raft ID. This Raft ID will appear while adding a node using `raft.addPeer`.

Now, let's remove a node from the network. Let's remove the third node from the `static-nodes.json` file. This node will have `raft` ID of 3. In the node 1's interactive console, run the following code to remove the third node from the network:

```
raft.removePeer(3)
```

Now, the third peer will be removed from the network. You can now use the `admin.peers` API to check the list of total nodes connected to this node. It should be two nodes in the list, a total of three nodes in the network.

> In case a node is down at the time of adding or removing a new node to the network, then the downed node will come to know about the changes to the network once it's up and running.

Building your first IBFT network

We will build a network of six nodes. The first four will be validators and the other two will be non-validators. We will not add a constellation in this network. If you want to add one, the instructions are the same as previously.

In IBFT, every validator is identified uniquely using an Ethereum account derived from its node key. Similar to Raft, in IBFT, before setting up the network you have to decide on the total number of validators that will be in the network and then generate an enode for each. And then, we create a `static-nodes.json` file listing the enodes of all the validating nodes, and feed this file to every validator in the network. After that, derive Ethereum addresses from the node IDs. And finally, we construct the `extraData` field and create the `genesis` file.

> In the case of IBFT, creating the `static-nodes.json` file is not necessary. You can connect nodes using the `admin.addPeer(url)` API too.

Installing IBFT tools

The IBFT software contains tools for configuring the IBFT network, generating enodes, generating addresses derived from the node key, creating genesis blocks, and so on. Creating a genesis block for IBFT is not as simple as creating it for Raft, as there is a encoded `extraData` field that needs to be included in the genesis block listing the list of validators.

Following are the steps to install IBFT tools:

```
cd ~
mkdir -p go/src/github.com/getamis
cd go/src/github.com/getamis
git clone https://github.com/getamis/istanbul-tools.git
export GOPATH=~/go
go get github.com/getamis/istanbul-tools/cmd/istanbul
cd ~/go/bin
```

Now, in the `~/go/bin` directory, you will find an executable file named `istanbul`. This is the tool to create the genesis block. Create a directory named `ibft` and move the executable there.

Creating a genesis block

IBFT tools can automate the creation of a genesis block. At the same time, it also generates node keys, addresses derived from node keys, and the `static-nodes.json` file.

Run the following command to generate all these:

```
./istanbul setup --num 4 --nodes --verbose
```

And now, you will get a similar output:

```
validators
{
     "Address": "0x05a6245732c2350ba2ed64e840394c2239f8ad1f",
     "Nodekey":
"eae5093e524bf14ba6e95c13591d6a785be9ea486b9e8e9c1281314f75a3d4f9",
     "NodeInfo":
"enode://bd1049d796f1b71bef17d428ce8db5f22e478ecbeb9513c57e90d93ca1e9ec107f
4f4b43585556ca8bb3ab630f1f6543d0d4147f5d890e1fde301b2af1fd7a08@0.0.0.0:3030
3?discport=0"
}
{
     "Address": "0x97a80dc7a7e27f41ae006fa1253f1f105f77335c",
```

```
    "Nodekey":
"decc1787fda1f4079511bcff92e83f868755c8e06636303c42cfb3cce554919e",
    "NodeInfo":
"enode://6344e12a9b3f4fd5c154ee13ebe5351a5460a44302fd493a5e742adf8a294b6dc1
12fab1fa8ff19dde0027373c96c51ab6254153877c9fadabfc057624e522f0@0.0.0.0:3030
3?discport=0"
}
{
    "Address":  "0xf69faf33e8690e82b0043e9131e09bbbc394cbed",
    "Nodekey":
"7e1a7660f4ec525096ebea34a7a3b78803138fbaaa3f61b7dc13439ce3e08c95",
    "NodeInfo":
"enode://0955966accd8f36256e876790c9b66098675f7ac6bfc10b805d7356d66844cf696
902b8dadb62c44cdb783db69197ebacc709ab1908229fe7e13be3f1eae35fe@0.0.0.0:3030
3?discport=0"
}
{
    "Address":  "0x68795d3e326b553dc8b2c5739b87a9cb827037c8",
    "Nodekey":
"9f0e0b268671c29c43a0976faa7e08fd20aae24219ad1db6dfc7e645413600c1",
    "NodeInfo":
"enode://a76bf5be8ddd1b1b9bd8d46e5947ccef9c1ce492d4e8fe800e234e61be67a0dbd5
86e33afb4e17998dc53fa2ea5c72a8a0544c7baae45fc4c16c401c1de90a22@0.0.0.0:3030
3?discport=0"
}
```

static-nodes.json

```
[
"enode://bd1049d796f1b71bef17d428ce8db5f22e478ecbeb9513c57e90d93ca1e9ec107f
4f4b43585556ca8bb3ab630f1f6543d0d4147f5d890e1fde301b2af1fd7a08@0.0.0.0:3030
3?discport=0",
"enode://6344e12a9b3f4fd5c154ee13ebe5351a5460a44302fd493a5e742adf8a294b6dc1
12fab1fa8ff19dde0027373c96c51ab6254153877c9fadabfc057624e522f0@0.0.0.0:3030
3?discport=0",
"enode://0955966accd8f36256e876790c9b66098675f7ac6bfc10b805d7356d66844cf696
902b8dadb62c44cdb783db69197ebacc709ab1908229fe7e13be3f1eae35fe@0.0.0.0:3030
3?discport=0",
"enode://a76bf5be8ddd1b1b9bd8d46e5947ccef9c1ce492d4e8fe800e234e61be67a0dbd5
86e33afb4e17998dc53fa2ea5c72a8a0544c7baae45fc4c16c401c1de90a22@0.0.0.0:3030
3?discport=0"
]
```

genesis.json

```
{
    "config": {
        "chainId": 2017,
        "homesteadBlock": 1,
        "eip150Block": 2,
```

```
        "eip150Hash":
"0x0000000000000000000000000000000000000000000000000000000000000000",
        "eip155Block": 3,
        "eip158Block": 3,
        "istanbul": {
            "epoch": 30000,
            "policy": 0
        }
    },
    "nonce": "0x0",
    "timestamp": "0x5a213583",
    "extraData":
"0x0000000000000000000000000000000000000000000000000000000000000f89af854
9405a6245732c2350ba2ed64e840394c2239f8ad1f9497a80dc7a7e27f41ae006fa1253f1f1
05f77335c94f69faf33e8690e82b0043e9131e09bbbc394cbed9468795d3e326b553dc8b2c5
739b87a9cb827037c8b84100000000000000000000000000000000000000000000000000000
0000000000000000000000000000000000000000000000000000000000000000000000000000
00c0",
    "gasLimit": "0x47b760",
    "difficulty": "0x1",
    "mixHash":
"0x63746963616c2062797a616e74696e65206661756c7420746f6c6572616e6365",
    "coinbase": "0x0000000000000000000000000000000000000000",
    "alloc": {
        "05a6245732c2350ba2ed64e840394c2239f8ad1f": {
            "balance": "0x446c3b15f9926687d2c40534fdb564000000000000"
        },
        "68795d3e326b553dc8b2c5739b87a9cb827037c8": {
            "balance": "0x446c3b15f9926687d2c40534fdb564000000000000"
        },
        "97a80dc7a7e27f41ae006fa1253f1f105f77335c": {
            "balance": "0x446c3b15f9926687d2c40534fdb564000000000000"
        },
        "f69faf33e8690e82b0043e9131e09bbbc394cbed": {
            "balance": "0x446c3b15f9926687d2c40534fdb564000000000000"
        }
    },
    "number": "0x0",
    "gasUsed": "0x0",
    "parentHash":
"0x0000000000000000000000000000000000000000000000000000000000000000"
}
```

You will see different addresses, enodes, and so on. Now, create the `static-nodes.json`, `genesis.json`, and enode key files and place the preceding content in it. Set the node key file names as `enode_id_1`, `enode_id_2`, `enode_id_3`, and `enode_id_1`. Change the ports in the enode URLs to `23000`, `23001`, `23002`, and `23003`.

Now, let's generate an Ethereum account, and in the genesis block assign some ether to it. Ether is not generated dynamically, therefore we need to pre-supply. Use the following command to generate an Ethereum account:

```
./geth --datadir ./accounts account new
```

Now, change the name of the file in `accounts/keystore` to `key1`. And then copy the address, put it in the `genesis` file, and assign some balance. For example, if my newly generated account's address is `0x65d8c00633404140986e5e23aa9de8ea689c1d05`, then my `genesis` file content will be as follows:

```
{
    "config": {
        "chainId": 2017,
        "homesteadBlock": 1,
        "eip150Block": 2,
        "eip150Hash":
            "0x00000000000000000000000000000000000000000
             00000000000000000000000",
        "eip155Block": 3,
        "eip158Block": 3,
        "istanbul": {
            "epoch": 30000,
            "policy": 0
        }
    },
    "nonce": "0x0",
    "timestamp": "0x5a213583",
    "extraData": "0x00000000000000000000000000000000000000000000000
        00000000000000000000f89af8549405a6245732c2350ba2ed64e840
        394c2239f8ad1f9497a80dc7a7e27f41ae006fa1253f1f105f77
        335c94f69faf33e8690e82b0043e9131e09bbbc394cbed9468795
        d3e326b553dc8b2c5739b87a9cb827037c8b841000000000000000
        00000000000000000000000000000000000000000000000
        00000000000000000000000000000000000000000000000
        0000000000000000000000c0",
    "gasLimit": "0x47b760",
    "difficulty": "0x1",
    "mixHash": "0x63746963616c2062797a616e74696e65206661756c7c7
        420746f6c6572616e6365",
    "coinbase": "0x0000000000000000000000000000000000000000",
    "alloc": {
        "05a6245732c2350ba2ed64e840394c2239f8ad1f": {
            "balance": "0x446c3b15f9926687d2c40534fdb564000000000000"
        },
        "68795d3e326b553dc8b2c5739b87a9cb827037c8": {
            "balance": "0x446c3b15f9926687d2c40534fdb564000000000000"
```

```
        },
        "97a80dc7a7e27f41ae006fa1253f1f105f77335c": {
            "balance": "0x446c3b15f9926687d2c40534fdb564000000000000000"
        },
        "f69faf33e8690e82b0043e9131e09bbbc394cbed": {
            "balance": "0x446c3b15f9926687d2c40534fdb564000000000000000"
        },
        "65d8c00633404140986e5e23aa9de8ea689c1d05": {
            "balance": "0x446c3b15f9926687d2c40534fdb564000000000000000"
        }
    },
    "number": "0x0",
    "gasUsed": "0x0",
    "parentHash": "0x00000000000000000000000000000000
      0000000000000000000000000000000000"
}
```

Starting nodes

Now, before we start the nodes, we need to initialize them: create data directories for each node, copy the account keys to the data directory, copy the enode keys of the validators, and Bootstrap the blockchain with the genesis block.

Following are the commands to achieve these for all six nodes:

```
#Configuring Node 1
mkdir -p qdata/node1/{keystore,geth}
cp accounts/keystore/key1 qdata/node1/keystore
cp static-nodes.json qdata/node1
cp enode_id_1 qdata/node1/geth/nodekey
./geth --datadir qdata/node1 init genesis.json

#Configuring Node 2
mkdir -p qdata/node2/geth
cp static-nodes.json qdata/node2
cp enode_id_2 qdata/node2/geth/nodekey
./geth --datadir qdata/node2 init genesis.json

#Configuring Node 3
mkdir -p qdata/node3/geth
cp static-nodes.json qdata/node3
cp enode_id_3 qdata/node3/geth/nodekey
./geth --datadir qdata/node3 init genesis.json

#Configuring Node 4
mkdir -p qdata/node4/geth
```

```
cp static-nodes.json qdata/node4
cp enode_id_4 qdata/node4/geth/nodekey
./geth --datadir qdata/node4 init genesis.json

#Configuring Node 5
mkdir -p qdata/node5/geth
cp static-nodes.json qdata/node5
./geth --datadir qdata/node5 init genesis.json

#Configuring Node 6
mkdir -p qdata/node6/geth
cp static-nodes.json qdata/node6
./geth --datadir qdata/node6 init genesis.json
```

The preceding commands are self-explanatory. For the last two nodes, we didn't generate any enode keys because `geth` will automatically generate the if one doesn't exist. Now, run the following commands to start the Quorum nodes. Run each command in a new shell window:

```
./geth --datadir qdata/node1 --mine --port 23000 --ipcpath "./geth.ipc" --istanbul.requesttimeout 5000 --istanbul.blockperiod 1 --istanbul.blockpausetime 20 console
./geth --datadir qdata/node2 --mine --port 23001 --ipcpath "./geth.ipc" --istanbul.requesttimeout 5000 --istanbul.blockperiod 1 --istanbul.blockpausetime 20 console
./geth --datadir qdata/node3 --mine --port 23002 --ipcpath "./geth.ipc" --istanbul.requesttimeout 5000 --istanbul.blockperiod 1 --istanbul.blockpausetime 20 console
./geth --datadir qdata/node4 --mine --port 23003 --ipcpath "./geth.ipc" --istanbul.requesttimeout 5000 --istanbul.blockperiod 1 --istanbul.blockpausetime 20 console
./geth --datadir qdata/node5 --port 23004 --ipcpath "./geth.ipc" console
./geth --datadir qdata/node6 --port 23005 --ipcpath "./geth.ipc" console
```

Here is the meaning of the different options we just passed:

- `--mine` is required while running the validators.
- `--istanbul.requesttimeout` is the maximum block time (`default: 10000ms`).
- `--istanbul.blockperiod` is the minimum block time (`default: 1s`).
- `--istanbul.blockpausetime` is the pause time when zero transactions in previous block. Values should be larger than `istanbul.blockperiod` (`default: 2s`).

To get a list of all validators in the network. you can use the `istanbul.getValidators()` API.

Adding or removing a validator dynamically

Let's first see how to add a new validator dynamically. To add a validator, we first need to generate the node key and address of the new validator. Run the following command to generate it:

```
./istanbul setup --num 1 --nodes --verbose
```

This is the same command we used earlier. Now, we don't need the `genesis` file or the `static-nodes.json` file. We just need the node key and address. Create a file named `node_id_5` and place the node key in it. Run the following commands to initialize the new validator:

```
#Configuring Node 7
mkdir -p qdata/node7/geth
cp static-nodes.json qdata/node7
cp enode_id_5 qdata/node7/geth/nodekey
./geth --datadir qdata/node7 init genesis.json
```

Now, after the preceding commands have run successfully, it's time for (*2F+ 1*) other validators to agree on the insertion of the new validator. For this, run the following command in all the other validators:

```
istanbul.propose("0x349ec6eefe8453a875c4905f5581ea792806a3e5", true)
```

Replace the first argument with the new validator's address you got. Now, start the new validator node using the following command:

```
./geth --datadir qdata/node7 --mine --port 23006 --ipcpath "./geth.ipc" --
istanbul.requesttimeout 5000 --istanbul.blockperiod 1 --
istanbul.blockpausetime 20 console
```

Now, you can run `istanbul.getValidators()` to check the list of all validators in the network. It should be five now. Let's remove a validator from the network. Let's assume that we want to remove the first validator. Run `eth.coinbase` in the console of the first validator to find its unique address. Then, run the following command in (*2F + 1*) validators to remove the first validator from the network:

```
istanbul.propose("0x05a6245732c2350ba2ed64e840394c2239f8ad1f", false)
```

Here, replace the first argument with the address of the first validator you generated.

 At the time of removing or adding a validator, if some validating node is down then it will automatically come to know about these changes once it's up and running.

Summary

In this chapter, we started with the basics of Ethereum blockchain in general, and then we jumped into the features and consensus protocols of Quorum. Then, we got our first hands-on with Quorum by setting up a constellation, Raft, and IBFT network. Now, you should be comfortable with the process of setting up a network. The next step is to learn about writing smart contracts, and deploy our first smart contracts. We will achieve this in the next chapter.

Writing Smart Contracts 3

In the previous chapter, we learned how Quorum works and how the various consensus protocols safeguard it. Let's move on to writing smart contracts, now that we understand how Quorum works. Quorum smart contracts can be written using many languages; the most popular one is **Solidity**. In this chapter, we will learn Solidity, and build a DApp that enterprises can use to sign documents digitally.

In this chapter, we'll cover the following topics:

- The layout of Solidity source files
- Understanding Solidity data types
- Special variables and contract functions
- Control structures
- Structure and features of contracts
- Compiling and deploying contracts

 This chapter is same as chapter present in author's previous book *Blockchain for Projects*. This is not a second edition book, it is used to explain fundamental concepts to the readers.

Solidity source files

You can identify a Solidity source file by the `.sol` extension. It has various versions, as programming languages usually do. The latest version at the time of writing this book is `0.4.17`.

In the source file, you can use the `pragma Solidity` directive to mention the compiler version for which the code is written. For example:

```
pragma Solidity ^0.4.17;
```

It is important to note that the source file will not compile with compiler versions earlier than `0.4.17` and later than `0.5.0` (this second condition is added using ^). Compiler versions between `0.4.17` and `0.5.0` are most likely to include bug fixes and less likely to break anything.

We can specify more complex rules for the compiler version; the expression follows those used by npm.

The structure of a smart contract

A is akin to a class. It can functions, modifiers, state variables, events, structures, and enums. Contracts also support inheritance. You can implement inheritance by copying code during compiling. Smart contracts can also be polymorphic.

The following an example of a smart contract:

```
contract Sample
{
    //state variables
    uint256 data;
    address owner;

    //event definition
    event logData(uint256 dataToLog);

    //function modifier
    modifier onlyOwner() {
        if (msg.sender != owner) throw;
        _;
    }

    //constructor
    function Sample(uint256 initData, address initOwner){
        data = initData;
        owner = initOwner;
    }

    //functions
    function getData() returns (uint256 returnedData){
        return data;
```

```
    }
    function setData(uint256 newData) onlyOwner{
        logData(newData);
        data = newData;
    }
}
```

Let's see how the aforementioned code works:

- First, we used the `contract` keyword to declare a contract.
- Next, we declared two state variables: `data` holds some data; and `owner` holds address of their Ethereum Wallet, that is, the address in which the contract was deployed. State variables form the state of the smart contract and it is stored in the storage of the smart contract. The storage of a smart contract is in the database.
- Then, we defined the event. Events are used for client notification. Our event will be triggered whenever data changes. All events are kept in the blockchain.
- Next, we defined a modifier function. Modifiers automatically check a condition before executing a function. Our modifier checks whether the contract owner is the one invoking the function. If not, then it will throw an exception.
- After that, we have the contract constructor. It is invoked while deploying the contract. The constructor is used to initialize the state variables.
- Finally, we defined two methods. The first method gets the value of the data state variable and the second changes the data value.

Before delving more deeply into smart contract features, there are some important things related to Solidity we must learn. After that, we will come back to contracts.

Data locations in Solidity

Unlike other programming languages, Solidity's variables are stored in the memory and the database, depending on the context.

There is always a default location, but it can be overridden for complex types of data, such as strings, arrays, and structs, by appending storage or memory to the type. Memory is the default for function parameters (including `return` parameters), and storage is for local and state variables (obviously).

Data locations are important because they change the behavior of assignments:

- An independent copy is always created for assignments between storage variables and memory variables. No copy is created, however, for assignments from one memory-stored complex type to another.
- An independent copy is always created for an assignment to a state variable (even from other state variables).
- Memory-stored complex types cannot be assigned to local storage variables.
- If state variables are assigned to local storage variables, the local storage variables point to the state variables; basically, local storage variables act as pointers.

The different types of data

Solidity is a statically-typed language; the type of data the variable holds needs to be predefined. All the bits of the variables are assigned to zero by default. In Solidity, variables are function-scoped; that is, a variable declared anywhere within a function will be in scope for the entire function regardless of where it is declared.

The following are the data types provided by Solidity:

- The most simple data type is `bool`. It can hold either `true` or `false`.
- `uint8`, `uint16`, `uint24`, up to `uint256` are used to hold unsigned integers of 8 bits, 16 bits, 24 bits, up to 256 bits, respectively. Similarly, `int8`, `int16` up to `int256` are used to hold signed integers of 8 bits, 16 bits up to 256 bits, respectively. `uint` and `int` are aliases for `uint256` and `int256`. `ufixed` and `fixed` represent fractional numbers. `ufixed0x8`, `ufixed0x16` up to `ufixed0x256` are used to hold unsigned fractional numbers of 8 bits, 16 bits up to 256 bits, respectively. Similarly, `fixed0x8`, `fixed0x16` up to `fixed0x256` are used to hold signed fractional numbers of 8 bits, 16 bits up to 256 bits, respectively. If we have a number that requires more than 256 bits, then the 256 bits data type is used, in which case the approximation of the number is stored.
- Address is used to store up to a 20-byte value by assigning a hexadecimal literal. It is used to store Ethereum addresses. You can use the `0x` prefix in Solidity to assign a hexadecimal encoded representation of values to variables.

Arrays

Solidity supports generic and byte arrays, fixed-size and dynamic arrays, as well as multidimensional arrays.

bytes1, bytes2, bytes3, **up to** , bytes32 are types of byte arrays. We will use byte to represent bytes1.

Here is an example of generic array syntaxes:

```
    contract sample{
//dynamic size array
//wherever an array literal is seen a new array is created. If the //array
literal is in state, then it's stored in storage and if it's //found inside
function, then its stored in memory
//Here myArray stores [0, 0] array. The type of [0, 0] is decided based
//on its values.
//Therefore, you cannot assign an empty array literal.
        int[] myArray = [0, 0];
        function sample(uint index, int value){
            //index of an array should be uint256 type
            myArray[index] = value;
            //myArray2 holds pointer to myArray
            int[] myArray2 = myArray;
//a fixed size array in memory
//here we are forced to use uint24 because 99999 is the max value and //24
bits is the max size required to hold it.
//This restriction is applied to literals in memory because memory is
//expensive. As [1, 2, 99999] is of type uint24, myArray3 also has to //be
the same type to store pointer to it.
            uint24[3] memory myArray3 = [1, 2, 99999]; //array literal

//throws exception while compiling as myArray4 cannot be assigned to
//complex type stored in memory
            uint8[2] myArray4 = [1, 2];
        }
}
```

The following are some important things you should know about arrays:

- Arrays also possess a length property that can be used to find the length of an array. value can also be assigned to the length property to change the array size. However, an array in memory or a non-dynamic array cannot be resized.
- An exception is thrown if an unset index of a dynamic array is accessed.

Strings

Strings can be created in Solidity in two ways: using `bytes` and `string`. `bytes` is used to create a raw string, whereas `string` is used to create a UTF-8 string. The length of the string is always dynamic.

Here is an example that shows `string` syntaxes:

```
contract sample {
//wherever a string literal is seen, a new string is created. If the
//string literal is in state, then it's stored in storage and if it's
//found inside function, then its stored in memory
    //Here myString stores "" string.
    string myString = ""; //string literal
    bytes myRawString;
    function sample(string initString, bytes rawStringInit){
        myString = initString;
        //myString2 holds a pointer to myString
        string myString2 = myString;

        //myString3 is a string in memory
        string memory myString3 = "ABCDE";

        //here the length and content changes
        myString3 = "XYZ";
        myRawString = rawStringInit;

        //incrementing the length of myRawString
        myRawString.length++;

        //throws exception while compiling
        string myString4 = "Example";

        //throws exception while compiling
        string myString5 = initString;
    }
}
```

Structs

Solidity structs. Here is an shows `struct` syntaxes:

```
contract sample{
    struct myStruct {
        bool myBool;
        string myString;
```

```
        }

    myStruct s1;
    //wherever a struct method is seen, a new struct is created. If
    //the struct method is in state, then it's stored in storage
    //and if it's found inside function, then its stored in memory
    myStruct s2 = myStruct(true, ""); //struct method syntax

    function sample(bool initBool, string initString){
        //create an instance of struct
        s1 = myStruct(initBool, initString);
        //myStruct(initBool, initString) creates an instance in memory
        myStruct memory s3 = myStruct(initBool, initString);
    }
}
```

Enums

Solidity enums. Here is an shows enum syntaxes:

```
contract sample {
    //The integer type which can hold all enum values and is the
    //smallest is chosen to hold enum values
    enum OS { Windows, Linux, OSX, UNIX }
    OS choice;
    function sample(OS chosen){
        choice = chosen;
    }

    function setLinuxOS(){
        choice = OS.Linux;
    }

    function getChoice() returns (OS chosenOS){
        return choice;
    }
}
```

Mappings

A **hash table** is a mapping data type. As mappings can only live in storage, they are declared as state variables. You can think of a mapping as having key and value pairs. key is not actually stored; instead, the **keccak256** hash of key is used to look up for value. Mappings don't have a length and cannot be assigned to another mapping.

Here is an example of creating and using `mapping`:

```
contract sample{
    mapping (int => string) myMap;
    function sample(int key, string value){
        myMap[key] = value;

        //myMap2 is a reference to myMap
        mapping (int => string) myMap2 = myMap;
    }
}
```

The delete operator

The `delete` operator can be applied to any variable to reset it to its default value. The default value is all bits assigned to zero.

If we apply `delete` to a dynamic array, it will delete all its elements and the length becomes zero. And if we apply it to a static array, all its indices are reset. We can also apply `delete` to specific indices, to reset them.

Nothing happens, though, if you apply `delete` to a map type. However, if you apply `delete` to `key` of a map, the value associated with `key` is deleted.

Let's see the `delete` operator at work, as follows:

```
contract sample {

    struct Struct {
        mapping (int => int) myMap;
        int myNumber;
    }

    int[] myArray;
    Struct myStruct;

    function sample(int key, int value, int number, int[] array) {

        //maps cannot be assigned so while constructing struct we
        // ignore the maps
        myStruct = Struct(number);

        //here set the map key/value
        myStruct.myMap[key] = value;
```

```
        myArray = array;
    }

function reset(){

        //myArray length is now 0
        delete myArray;

        //myNumber is now 0 and myMap remains as it is
        delete myStruct;
    }

function deleteKey(int key){

        //here we are deleting the key
        delete myStruct.myMap[key];
    }
}
```

Conversion between elementary types

Everything apart from arrays, strings, structs, enums, and maps is called **elementary types**.

If we apply an operator to different types, the compiler tries to implicitly convert one of the operands into the type of the other. Generally speaking, an implicit conversion between value types is possible if it makes sense semantically and no information is lost: uint8 is convertible to uint16, and int128 to int256, but int8 is not convertible to uint256 (because uint256 cannot hold, for example, -1). Furthermore, an unsigned integer can be converted into a byte of the same or a larger size, but not the reverse. Any type that can be converted into uint160 can also be converted into an address.

Solidity also supports explicit conversion. You can opt for explicit conversion if the compiler does not allow implicit conversion between two data types. We recommend avoiding an explicit conversion as it may give you unexpected results.

The following example of explicit conversion, as follows:

```
uint32 a = 0x12345678;
uint16 b = uint16(a); // b will be 0x5678 now
```

Here, we are converting the uint32 type to uint16 explicitly, that is, converting a large type to a smaller type; therefore, higher-order bits are cut off.

Using var

To declare variables, Solidity provides the var keyword. The type of variable in this case is decided dynamically, depending on the first value assigned to it. Once a value is assigned, the type is fixed; if you assign another type to it, it will lead to type conversion.

Let's see how var works, as follows:

```
int256 x = 12;

//y type is int256
var y = x;

uint256 z= 9;

//exception because implicit conversion not possible
y = z;
```

 Note that var cannot be used when defining arrays and maps. It also cannot be used to define function parameters and state variables.

Control structures

Solidity supports if...else, do...while, for, break, continue, return, and ?: control structures.

Here a of structures:

```
contract sample{
    int a = 12;
    int[] b;

    function sample()
    {
        //"==" throws exception for complex types
        if(a == 12)
        {
        }
        else if(a == 34)
        {
        }
        else
        {
```

```
        }

        var temp = 10;

        while(temp < 20)
        {
            if(temp == 17)
            {
                break;
            }
            else
            {
                continue;
            }

            temp++;
        }

        for(var iii = 0; iii < b.length; iii++)
        {

        }
    }
}
```

Creating contracts using the new operator

A contract can create a new contract using the new keyword . The complete code for the contract being created must be known.

Let's demonstrate, as follows:

```
contract sample1
{
    int a;

    function assign(int b)
    {
        a = b;
    }
}


contract sample2{
    function sample2()
    {
```

```
        sample1 s = new sample1();
        s.assign(12);
    }
}
```

Exceptions

In some cases, exceptions are thrown automatically. You can use `assert()`, `revert()`, and `require()` to throw manual exceptions. Exceptions stop and revert any currently-executing calls (that is, all changes to the state and balances are undone). In Solidity, it is not yet possible to catch exceptions.

The following three lines are all different ways of throwing exceptions in Solidity:

```
if(x != y) { revert(); }

//In assert() and require(), the conditional statement is an inversion //to
"if" block's condition, switching the comparison operator != to ==
assert(x == y);
require(x == y);
```

`assert()` will take away all the gas, whereas `require()` and `revert()` will refund the remaining gas.

Solidity doesn't support returning a reason for exceptions but is expected to soon. You can visit the `https://github.com/ethereum/solidity/issues/1686`https://github.com/ethereum/solidity/issues/1686 issue for an update. Then you will be able to write `revert("Something bad happened")` and `require(condition, "Something bad happened")`.

External function calls

Solidity has two kinds of function calls: internal and external. An internal function call is when a function calls another function in the same contract. An external function call is when a function calls a function of another contract.

The following an example:

```
contract sample1
{
    int a;
```

```
//"payable" is a built-in modifier
//This modifier is required if another contract is sending
// Ether while calling the method
function sample1(int b) payable
{
    a = b;
}

function assign(int c)
{
    a = c;
}

function makePayment(int d) payable
{
    a = d;
}
}


contract sample2{

function hello()
{
}

function sample2(address addressOfContract)
{
    //send 12 wei while creating contract instance
    sample1 s = (new sample1).value(12)(23);

    s.makePayment(22);

    //sending Ether also
    s.makePayment.value(45)(12);

    //specifying the amount of gas to use
    s.makePayment.gas(895)(12);

    //sending Ether and also specifying gas
    s.makePayment.value(4).gas(900)(12);

    //hello() is internal call whereas this.hello() is
    external call
    this.hello();

    //pointing a contract that's already deployed
    sample1 s2 = sample1(addressOfContract);
```

```
        s2.makePayment(112);


    }
}
```

 Calls made using the `this` keyword are called external calls. The `this` keyword inside functions represents the current contract instance.

Features of contracts

It is time to delve more deeply into contracts. Let's start with some new features and then we will go deeper into the features we have already seen.

Visibility

The visibility of a state variable or a function defines who can see it. There are four kinds of visibility: `external`, `public`, `internal`, and `private`.

By default, the visibility of functions is `public` and the visibility of state variables is `internal`. Let's see what these visibility functions mean:

- `external`: External functions can only be called from other contracts or via transactions. For example, we cannot call an `f` external function internally: `f()` will not work but `this.f()` will. We also cannot apply `external` visibility to state variables.
- `public`: Public functions and state variables can be accessed in every possible way. Compiler-generated accessor functions are all `public` state variables. It is not possible to create our own accessors. Actually, it generates only **getters**, not **setters**.
- `internal`: Internal functions and state variables can only be accessed internally, that is, from within the current contract and the contracts inheriting it. We cannot use `this` to access it.
- `private`: Private functions and state variables are similar to internal ones, except they cannot be accessed by the inheriting contracts.

Here is a code example to demonstrate visibility and accessors:

```
contract sample1
{
    int public b = 78;
    int internal c = 90;

    function sample1()
    {
        //external access
        this.a();

        //compiler error
        a();

        //internal access
        b = 21;

        //external access
        this.b;

        //external access
        this.b();

        //compiler error
        this.b(8);

        //compiler error
        this.c();

        //internal access
        c = 9;
    }

    function a() external
    {

    }
}

contract sample2
{
    int internal d = 9;
    int private e = 90;
}

//sample3 inherits sample2
contract sample3 is sample2
```

```
{
    sample1 s;

    function sample3()
    {
        s = new sample1();

        //external access
        s.a();

        //external access
        var f = s.b;

        //compiler error as accessor cannot used to assign a value
        s.b = 18;

        //compiler error
        s.c();

        //internal access
        d = 8;

        //compiler error
        e = 7;
    }
}
```

Function modifiers

We have already seen what a function modifier is, and we wrote a basic version of it. Now let's look at it in detail.

Modifiers are inherited by child contracts, and they can also be overridden by child contracts. Multiple modifiers can be applied to a function by specifying them in a whitespace-separated list and they will be evaluated in order. You can also pass arguments to modifiers.

Inside the modifier, the next modifier body or function body, whichever comes next, is inserted where _; appears.

Let's take a look at a complex code example of function modifiers, as follows:

```
contract sample
{
    int a = 90;
```

```
modifier myModifier1(int b) {
    int c = b;
    _;
    c = a;
    a = 8;
}

modifier myModifier2 {
    int c = a;
    _;
}

modifier myModifier3 {
    a = 96;
    return;
    _;
    a = 99;
}

modifier myModifier4 {
    int c = a;
    _;
}

function myFunction() myModifier1(a) myModifier2 myModifier3 returns
(int d)
{
    a = 1;
    return a;
}
}
```

This is how myFunction() is executed:

```
int c = b;
    int c = a;
        a = 96;
        return;
            int c = a;
                a = 1;
                return a;
        a = 99;
c = a;
a = 8;
```

Here, when you call the myFunction method, it will return 0. But after that, when you try to access the state variable, a, you will get 8.

`return` in a modifier or function body immediately leaves the whole function, and the return value is assigned to whatever variable it needs to be.

In the case of functions, the code after `return` is executed after the caller's code-execution is completed. And in the case of modifiers, the code after _; in the previous modifier is executed after the caller's code-execution is completed. In the aforementioned example, line numbers five, six, and seven are never executed. After line number four, the execution starts directly from line numbers eight to ten.

`return` inside modifiers cannot have a value associated with it. It always returns zero bits.

The fallback function

The **fallback function** is the only unnamed function a contract can have. This function cannot have arguments and cannot return anything. It is executed on a call to the contract if none of the other functions match the given function identifier.

This function is also executed whenever the contract receives Ether without any function call; that is, the transaction sends Ethereum to the contracts and doesn't invoke any method. In such a context, there is usually very little gas available for the function call (precisely 2,300 gas), so it is important to make fallback functions as cheap as possible.

Contracts throw an exception when they receive Ether but do not have a defined fallback function, thereby sending back the Ether. So if you want your contract to receive Ethereum, you must implement a fallback function.

Here is an example of a fallback function:

```
contract sample
{
    function() payable
    {
        //Note how much Ether has been sent and by whom
    }
}
```

Inheritance

Solidity supports multiple inheritance by copying code, including polymorphism. Even if a contract inherits from multiple other contracts, only a single contract will be created on the blockchain. Moreover, the code from the parent contracts will always be copied into the final contract.

Let's review an example of inheritance:

```
contract sample1
{
    function a(){}

    function b(){}
}


//sample2 inherits sample1
contract sample2 is sample1
{
    function b(){}
}

contract sample3
{
    function sample3(int b)
    {

    }
}

//sample4 inherits from sample1 and sample2
//Note that sample1 is also a parent of sample2; yet there is only a
// single instance of sample1
contract sample4 is sample1, sample2
{
    function a(){}

    function c(){

        //this executes the "a" method of sample3 contract
        a();

        //this executes the "a" method of sample1 contract
        sample1.a();

        //calls sample2.b() because it is last in the parent
        contracts list and therefore it overrides sample1.b()
        b();
    }
}

//If a constructor takes an argument, it needs to be provided at
//the constructor of the child contract.
//In Solidity, child constructor does not call parent constructor,
```

```
// instead parent is initialized and copied to child
contract sample5 is sample3(122)
{

}
```

The super keyword

The super keyword is used to refer to the next contract in the final inheritance chain. The following is an example to help you understand it better:

```
contract sample1
{
}

contract sample2
{
}

contract sample3 is sample2
{
}

contract sample4 is sample2
{
}

contract sample5 is sample4
{
    function myFunc()
    {
    }
}

contract sample6 is sample1, sample2, sample3, sample5
{
    function myFunc()
    {
        //sample5.myFunc()
        super.myFunc();
    }
}
```

The final inheritance chain with respect to the sample6 contract is sample6, sample5, sample4, sample2, sample3, sample1. The inheritance chain starts with the most-derived contracts and ends with the least-derived contract.

Abstract contracts

Abstract contracts are those that only contain the prototype of functions instead of the implementation. They cannot be compiled (even if they contain implemented functions alongside non-implemented functions). If a contract inherits from an abstract contract and does not implement all non-implemented functions by overriding, it will itself become abstract.

The reason abstract contracts are provided is to make the interface known to the compiler. This is useful for referring to a deployed contract and calling its functions.

Let's demonstrate this, as follows:

```
contract sample1
{
    function a() returns (int b);
}


contract sample2
{
    function myFunc()
    {
        sample1 s =
          sample1(0xd5f9d8d94886e70b06e474c3fb14fd43e2f23970);

        //without abstract contract this wouldn't have compiled
        s.a();
    }
}
```

Libraries

Libraries are similar to contracts, but they are deployed just once at a specific address and their code is reused by various contracts. This means that if library functions are called, their code is executed in the context of the calling contract; So, `this` points to the calling contract, and specifically, allows access to the storage from the calling contract. As a library is an isolated piece of source code, it can only access state variables of the calling contract if they are explicitly supplied (it would have no way to name them otherwise).

Libraries can contain structs and enums, but they cannot have state variables. They don't support inheritance and they cannot receive Ethereum.

Once a Solidity library is deployed to the blockchain, it can be used by anyone, assuming one knows its address and has the source code (with only prototypes or complete implementation). The source code is required by the Solidity compiler so it can ensure that the methods being accessed actually exist in the library.

Here is an example:

```
library math
{
    function addInt(int a, int b) returns (int c)
    {
        return a + b;
    }
}

contract sample
{
    function data() returns (int d)
    {
        return math.addInt(1, 2);
    }
}
```

The address of the library cannot be added in the contract source code. We need to provide the library address to the compiler during compilation.

Libraries have many use cases. The two major use cases are as follows:

- If you have several contracts with some common code, you can deploy that common code as a library. This will save gas, which also depends on the contract size. Therefore, we can think of a library as a base contract of the contract that uses it. Using a base contract instead of a library to split the common code will not save gas, because inheritance in Solidity works by copying code. Because libraries are thought of as base contracts, functions with internal visibility in a library are copied to the contract that uses it. Otherwise, functions with the `internal` visibility of a library cannot be called by the contract that uses the library, as an external call would be required. Functions with the `internal` visibility cannot be invoked using the external call. In addition, structs and enums in a library are copied to the contract that uses the library.
- Libraries can be used to add member functions to data types.

 A library containing only internal functions and/or structs/enums does not need to be deployed, as everything that's in the library is copied to the contract that uses it.

using for

The using A for B; directive can be used to attach library functions (from the library, A, to any type, B). These functions will receive the object they are called on as their first parameter.

The effect of using A for *; is that the functions from the library, A, are attached to all types.

Here is an example to demonstrate for:

```
library math
{
    struct myStruct1 {
        int a;
    }

    struct myStruct2 {
        int a;
    }

    //Here we have to make 's' location storage so that we
    //get a reference.
    //Otherwise addInt will end up accessing/modifying a
    //different instance of myStruct1 than the one on which its invoked
    function addInt(myStruct1 storage s, int b) returns (int c)
    {
        return s.a + b;
    }

    function subInt(myStruct2 storage s, int b) returns (int c)
    {
        return s.a + b;
    }
}

contract sample
{
    //"*" attaches the functions to all the structs
    using math for *;
    math.myStruct1 s1;
    math.myStruct2 s2;

    function sample()
    {
        s1 = math.myStruct1(9);
        s2 = math.myStruct2(9);
```

```
        s1.addInt(2);

        //compiler error as the first parameter of addInt is
        //of type myStruct1 so addInt is not attached to myStruct2
        s2.addInt(1);
    }
}
```

Returning multiple values

Solidity allows functions to return multiple values. Let's demonstrate this, as follows:

```
contract sample
{
    function a() returns (int a, string c)
    {
        return (1, "ss");
    }

    function b()
    {
        int A;
        string memory B;

        //A is 1 and B is "ss"
        (A, B) = a();

        //A is 1
        (A,) = a();

        //B is "ss"
        (, B) = a();
    }
}
```

Importing other Solidity source files

Solidity allows a source file to import other source files. Here is an example to demonstrate this:

```
//This statement imports all global symbols from "filename" (and //symbols
imported therein) to the current global scope. "filename" can //be an
absolute or relative path. It can only be an HTTP URL
//import "filename";
```

```
//creates a new global symbol symbolName whose members are all the //global
symbols from "filename".
import * as symbolName from "filename";

//creates new global symbols alias and symbol2 which reference symbol1
//and symbol2 from "filename", respectively.
import {symbol1 as alias, symbol2} from "filename";

//this is equivalent to import * as symbolName from "filename";.
import "filename" as symbolName;
```

Globally-available variables

There are special variables and functions that always exist globally. We will discuss them in upcoming sections.

Block and transaction properties

The block and transaction properties are as follows:

- `block.blockhash(uint blockNumber) returns (bytes32)`: The hash of the given block only works for the 256 most recent blocks.
- `block.coinbase (address)`: The current block's miner's address.
- `block.difficulty (uint)`: The current block's difficulty.
- `block.gaslimit (uint)`: The current block's gas limit. It defines the maximum amount of gas that all transactions in the whole block combined are allowed to consume. Its purpose is to keep the block-propagation and processing time low, thereby allowing a sufficiently decentralized network. Miners have the right to set the gas limit for the current block to be within ~0.0975% (1/1,024) of the gas limit of the last block, so the resulting gas limit should be the median of the miners' preferences.
- `block.number (uint)`: The current block's number.
- `block.timestamp (uint)`: The current block's timestamp.
- `msg.data (bytes)`: The complete call data holds the function and its arguments that the transaction invokes.
- `msg.gas (uint)`: The remaining gas.
- `msg.sender (address)`: The sender of the message (the current call).
- `msg.sig (bytes4)`: The first four bytes of the call data (the function identifier).

- `msg.value (uint)`: The number of wei sent with the message.
- `now (uint)`: The current block's timestamp (alias for block.timestamp).
- `tx.gasprice (uint)`: The gas price of the transaction.
- `tx.origin (address)`: The sender of the transaction (full call chain).

Address-type-related variables

Address-type-related variables are as follows:

- `<address>.balance (uint256)`: The balance of the address in wei.
- `<address>.send(uint256 amount) returns (bool)`: Sends the given amount of wei to `address`; returns `false` on failure. Even if the execution fails, the current contract will not stop with an exception.
- `<address>.transfer(uint256 amount)`: Sends wei to an address. If that execution runs out of gas or fails, the Ether transfer will be reversed and the current contract will stop with an exception.

Contract-related variables

Contract-related variables are as follows:

- `this`: The current contract, explicitly convertible to the address type
- `selfdestruct(address recipient)`: Destroys the current contract, sending its funds to the given address

Ether units

A literal number can take a suffix of `wei`, `finney`, `szabo`, or `ether` to convert between the sub-denominations of Ether, where Ether currency numbers without a postfix are assumed to be wei. For example, `2 Ether == 2000 finney` evaluates to `true`.

Proof of existence, integrity, and ownership contract

Nowadays, enterprises are using electronic signature solutions to sign agreements. However, the details of such files are stored in databases that can be changed easily, so they cannot be trusted for auditing purposes. Blockchain can solve this issue by integrating blockchain as a solution for these electronic signature systems.

Let's write a Solidity contract that can prove file ownership without revealing the actual file. It can prove that the file existed at a particular time and check for file integrity.

Enterprises can use this solution to store a hash of their agreements on blockchain. The advantage of doing this on blockchains is that the agreement date/time, the actual terms of the agreement, and so on can be proven.

We will achieve proof of ownership by storing the hash of the file and the owner's name as pairs. The owner can be the enterprise that created the agreement. On the other hand, we will achieve proof of existence by storing the hash of the file and the block timestamp as pairs. Finally, storing the hash itself proves the integrity of the file. If the file is modified, its hash will change and the contract won't be able to find the file, thereby proving that the file was modified.

We will use Quorum's private transactions because agreements signed between entities are private to them and details are not exposed to other entities. Although only the hash of the file will be exposed, it's still not a good idea for other entities to know how many agreements an entity is signing.

Here is the code for the smart contract to achieve all this:

```
contract Proof
{
 struct FileDetails
 {
 uint timestamp;
 string owner;
 }

 mapping (string => FileDetails) files;

 event logFileAddedStatus(bool status, uint timestamp,
   string owner, string fileHash);

 //this is used to store the owner of file at the block timestamp
 function set(string owner, string fileHash)
```

```
{
//There is no proper way to check if a key already exists,
//therefore we are checking for default value i.e., all bits are 0
if(files[fileHash].timestamp == 0)
{
files[fileHash] = FileDetails(block.timestamp, owner);

//we are triggering an event so that the frontend of our app
//knows that the file's existence and ownership
//details have been stored
logFileAddedStatus(true, block.timestamp, owner, fileHash);
}
else
{
//this tells the frontend that the file's existence and
//ownership details couldn't be stored because the
//file's details had already been stored earlier
logFileAddedStatus(false, block.timestamp, owner, fileHash);
}
}

//this is used to get file information
function get(string fileHash) returns (uint timestamp, string owner)
{
return (files[fileHash].timestamp, files[fileHash].owner);
}
}
```

Compiling and deploying contracts

Ethereum provides the solc compiler, which provides a command-line interface to compile .sol files. Visit http://solidity.readthedocs.io/en/develop/installing-solidity.html#binary-packages to find instructions on how to install it and visit https://Solidity.readthedocs.io/en/develop/using-the-compiler.html to find instructions on how to use it. We won't be using the solc compiler directly; instead, we will be using browser Solidity. Browser Solidity is an IDE, which is suitable for small contracts.

For now, let's just compile the preceding contract using browser Solidity. Learn more about it at https://Ethereum.github.io/browser-Solidity/. You can also download the browser Solidity source code for offline use: https://github.com/Ethereum/browser-Solidity/tree/gh-pages.

A major advantage of using browser Solidity is that it provides an editor and also generates code to deploy the contract.

In the editor, copy and paste the preceding contract code. You will see that it compiles and gives you the web3.js code to deploy it using the Geth interactive console.

You will get the following output without the `privateFor` property:

```
var proofContract =
web3.eth.contract([{"constant":false,"inputs":[{"name":"fileHash","type":"s
tring"}],"name":"get","outputs":[{"name":"timestamp","type":"uint256"},{"na
me":"owner","type":"string"}],"payable":false,"type":"function"},{"constant
":false,"inputs":[{"name":"owner","type":"string"},{"name":"fileHash","type
":"string"}],"name":"set","outputs":[],"payable":false,"type":"function"},{
"anonymous":false,"inputs":[{"indexed":false,"name":"status","type":"bool"}
,{"indexed":false,"name":"timestamp","type":"uint256"},{"indexed":false,"na
me":"owner","type":"string"},{"indexed":false,"name":"fileHash","type":"str
ing"}],"name":"logFileAddedStatus","type":"event"}]);
var proof = proofContract.new(
   {
     from: web3.eth.accounts[0],
     data: '0x606060.......',
     gas: 4700000,
   privateFor: ['CGXyBlYOGgU4fZ7n8dVLaTW24p+ZOF8kSiUJkQCUABk=',
     'zumojc44Dge0juFgph4xzqOUyNVw+QNZUaY7wOL0P0o=']
   }, function (e, contract){
    console.log(e, contract);
   if (typeof contract.address !== 'undefined') {
     console.log('Contract mined! address: ' + contract.address + '
       transactionHash: ' + contract.transactionHash);
   }
})
```

`data` represents the compiled version of the contract (bytecode) that the EVM understands. The source code is first converted into opcodes, which are then converted into bytecode. Each opcode has `gas` associated with it.

The first argument to `web3.eth.contract` is the ABI definition. The ABI definition contains the prototype of all the methods and is used when creating transactions.

Now it's time to deploy the smart contract. Before going further, make sure that you start the raft network we created in the last chapter with three nodes. We will assume the three nodes are of three different enterprises. Also make sure you have constellation enabled, and copy the public keys of all the constellation members. In the `privateFor` array, replace the public keys with the ones you generated. Here I am making the private smart contract visible to all the three network members.

privateFor is only used when sending a private transaction. It's assigned to an array of the recipients' base64-encoded public keys. In the preceding code, in the privateFor array, I only have two public keys. That's because the sender doesn't have to add its public key to the array. If you add it, then it will throw an error.

In the interactive console of the first node, unlock the Ethereum account, indefinitely, using personal.unlockAccount(web3.eth.accounts[0], "", 0).

On the right-hand panel of browser Solidity, copy everything that's there in the web3 deploy textarea, then add privateFor and paste it in the interactive console of the first node. Now press *Enter*. You will first get the transaction hash, and after waiting for some time, you will get the contract address after the transaction is mined. The transaction hash is the hash of the transaction, which is unique for every transaction. Every deployed contract has a unique contract address to identify the contract in the blockchain.

The contract address is deterministically computed from the address of its creator (the from address) and the number of transactions the creator has sent (the transaction nonce). These two are RLP-encoded and then hashed using the keccak256 hashing algorithm. We will learn more about the transaction nonce later. You can learn more about **Recursive Length Prefix (RLP)** at https://github.com/Ethereum/wiki/wiki/RLP.

Now let's store the file details and retrieve them. Assume that the first two entities have signed an agreement and want to store the file's details on the blockchain. Place this code to broadcast a transaction to store a file's details:

```
var contract_obj = proofContract.at
  ("0x006c3e992b6e3f52e81560aa3ef6d66e1706b45c");
contract_obj.set.sendTransaction("Enterprise 1",
  "e3b0c44298fc1c149afbf4c8996fb92427ae41e4649b934ca495991b7852b855"
  {
from: web3.eth.accounts[0],
privateFor: ['CGXyBlYOGgU4fZ7n8dVLaTW24p+ZOF8kSiUJkQCUABk=']
}, function(error, transactionHash){
  if (!err)
    console.log(transactionHash);
})
```

Here, replace the contract address with the contract address you got. The first argument of the `proofContract.at` method is the contract address. Here, we didn't provide the gas, in which case it's automatically calculated. And finally, as this is an agreement between first two entities and the first entity is sending the transaction with the second entity's public key, we have the public key of the second entity in the `privateFor` property.

Now run this code in order to find the file's details:

```
contract_obj.get.call("e3b0c44298fc1c149afbf4c8996fb92427ae41e4649b934c
    a495991b7852b855");
```

You will get this output:

```
[1477591434, "Owner Name"]
```

The call method is used to call a contract's method on EVM with the current state. It doesn't broadcast a transaction. To read data, we don't need to broadcast because we will have our own copy of the blockchain.

And if you run the preceding code in node 3, then you will not get any details because the data is not visible to the third entity. But the first and second node can read the details. We will learn more about web3.js in the coming chapters.

Summary

In this chapter, we learned about the Solidity programming language. We learned about data location, data types, and advanced features of contracts. We also learned the quickest and easiest way to compile and deploy a smart contract. Now you should be comfortable with writing smart contracts.

In the next chapter, we will build a frontend for the smart contract, which will make it easy to deploy the smart contract and run transactions.

Getting Started with web3.js 4

In the previous chapter, we learned how to write and deploy smart contracts using Solidity. In this chapter, we will learn about **web3.js** and how to import it, connect to geth, and use it in Node.js or client-side JavaScript. We will also learn how to build a web client using web3.js for the smart contract that we created in the previous chapter.

In this chapter, we'll cover the following topics:

- Importing web3.js in Node.js and client-side JavaScript
- Connecting to geth
- Exploring web3.js
- Discovering the most-used APIs of web3.js
- Building a Node.js application for an ownership contract

 This chapter is same as chapter present in author's previous book *Blockchain for Projects*. This is not a second edition book,it is used to explain fundamental concepts to the readers.

Introduction to web3.js

web3.js provides us with JavaScript APIs to communicate with geth. It uses JSON-RPC internally to communicate with geth. web3.js can also communicate with any other kind of Ethereum node that supports JSON-RPC. It exposes all JSON-RPC APIs as JavaScript APIs. It doesn't just support all the Ethereum-related APIs, but also supports APIs related to **Whisper** and **Swarm**.

As we build various projects, you will keep learning more about web3.js. For now, though, let's go through some of the most used APIs for web3.js. Later, we will build a frontend for our ownership smart contract using web3.js.

At the time of writing, the latest version of web3.js is 1.0.0-beta.18. We will learn everything using this version.

web3.js is hosted at `https://github.com/ethereum/web3.js` and the complete documentation is hosted at `https://github.com/ethereum/wiki/wiki/JavaScript-API`.

Importing web3.js

Simply run `npm install web3` inside your project directory to use web3.js in Node.js. In the source code, you can import it using `require("web3");`.

To use web3.js in client-side JavaScript, you can enqueue the `web3.js` file, which can be found inside the `dist` directory of the project source code. Now, the `web3` object will be available globally.

Connecting to nodes

web3.js can communicate with nodes using HTTP or IPC, and allows us to connect with multiple nodes. We will use HTTP for our node communication. An instance of `web3` represents a connection with a node. The instance exposes the APIs.

When an app is running inside mist, it automatically makes an instance of `web3` available that is connected to the mist node. The variable name of the instance is `web3`.

Here is the basic code to connect to a node:

```
if (typeof web3 !== 'undefined') {
   web3 = new Web3(new
Web3.providers.HttpProvider("http://localhost:8545"));
}
```

First, we verify whether the code is running inside mist by checking whether `web3` is `undefined` or not. If `web3` is defined, then we use the already available instance; otherwise, we create an instance by connecting to our custom node. You can remove the `if` condition from the preceding code if you want to connect to the custom node, regardless of whether or not the app is running inside mist. Here, we assume that our custom node is running locally on port number `8545`.

The `Web3.providers` object exposes constructors (called `providers` in this context) to establish a connection and transfer messages using various protocols. `Web3.providers.HttpProvider` lets us establish an HTTP connection, whereas `Web3.providers.IpcProvider` lets us establish an IPC connection.

The `web3.currentProvider` property is automatically assigned to the current provider instance. After creating a `web3` instance, you can change its provider using the `web3.setProvider()` method. It takes one argument, that is, the instance of the new provider.

> Remember that geth has HTTP-RPC disabled by default. So enable it by passing the `--rpc` option while running geth. HTTP-RPC runs on port `8545` by default.

`web3` exposes an `isConnected()` method that can be used to check whether or not it's connected to the node. It returns a `true` or `false` value depending on the connection status.

The API structure

`web3` contains an `eth` object (`web3.eth`) specifically for Ethereum blockchain interactions and an `shh` object (`web3.shh`) for Whisper interaction. Most web3.js APIs are inside these two objects.

All the APIs are synchronous by default. For an asynchronous request, you can pass an optional callback as the last parameter for most functions. All callbacks use an error-first callback style.

Some APIs have an alias for asynchronous requests. For example, `web3.eth.coinbase()` is synchronous, whereas `web3.eth.getCoinbase()` is asynchronous.

Here is an example:

```
//sync request
try
{
  console.log(web3.eth.getBlock(48));
}
catch(e)
{
  console.log(e);
}
```

```
//async request
web3.eth.getBlock(48, function(error, result){
    if(!error)
        console.log(result)
    else
        console.error(error);
})
```

`getBlock` is used to get information on a block using its number or hash. Or, it can take a string such as `"earliest"` (the genesis block), `"latest"` (the top block of the blockchain), or `"pending"` (the block that's being mined). If you don't pass an argument, then the default is `web3.eth.defaultBlock`, which is assigned to `"latest"` by default.

All of the APIs that need a block identification as an input can take a number, hash, or one of the readable strings. These APIs use `web3.eth.defaultBlock` by default if the value is not passed.

BigNumber.js

JavaScript is natively poor at handling big numbers. Therefore, for applications that require you to deal with big numbers and need perfect calculations, use the **BigNumber.js** library.

web3.js also depends on BigNumber.js and adds it automatically. web3.js always returns the `BigNumber` object for number values. It can take JavaScript numbers, number strings, and `BigNumber` instances as input.

Let's demonstrate this, as follows:

```
web3.eth.getBalance("0x27E829fB34d14f3384646F938165dfcD30cFfB7c")
    .toString();
```

Here, we use the `web3.eth.getBalance()` method to get the balance of an address. This method returns a `BigNumber` object. We need to call `toString()` on a `BigNumber` object to convert it into a number string.

BigNumber.js fails to correctly handle numbers with more than 20 floating point digits. Therefore, it is recommended that you store the balance in a wei unit, and while it is displayed, convert it to other units. web3.js itself always returns and takes the balance in wei. For example, the `getBalance()` method returns the balance of the address in the wei unit.

Unit conversion

web3.js provides APIs to convert the wei balance into any other unit and vice versa.

The `web3.fromWei()` method converts a wei number into another unit, whereas the `web3.toWei()` method converts a number in any other unit into wei. Here is an example to demonstrate this:

```
web3.fromWei("1000000000000000000", "ether");
web3.toWei("0.000000000000000001", "ether");
```

In the first line, we convert wei into `ether`; in the second line, we convert `ether` into wei. The second argument in both methods can be one of these strings:

- `kwei` or `ada`
- `mwei` or `babbage`
- `gwei` or `shannon`
- `szabo`
- `finney`
- `ether`
- `kether` / `grand` / `einstein`
- `mether`
- `gether`
- `tether`

Retrieving gas price, balance, and transaction details

Let's take a look at the APIs to retrieve the gas price, the balance of an address, and information on a mined transaction:

```
//It's sync. For async use getGasPrice
console.log(web3.eth.gasPrice.toString());

console.log(web3.eth.getBalance("0x407d73d8a49eeb85d32cf465507dd71d5071
   00c1", 45).toString());

console.log(web3.eth.getTransactionReceipt("0x9fc76417374aa880d4449a1f7
   f31ec597f00b1f6f3dd2d66f4c9c6c445836d8b"));
```

The output will be in this format:

```
20000000000
30000000000
{
  "transactionHash":
"0x9fc76417374aa880d4449a1f7f31ec597f00b1f6f3dd2d66f4c9c6c445836d8b ",
  "transactionIndex": 0,
  "blockHash":
"0xef95f2f1ed3ca60b048b4bf67cde2195961e0bba6f70bcbea9a2c4e133e34b46",
  "blockNumber": 3,
  "contractAddress": "0xa94f5374fce5edbc8e2a8697c15331677e6ebf0b",
  "cumulativeGasUsed": 314159,
  "gasUsed": 30234
}
```

The following is how the preceding method works:

- `web3.eth.gasPrice()`: Determines the gas price by the x latest blocks' median gas price.
- `web3.eth.getBalance()`: Returns the balance of any given address. All the hashes should be provided as hexadecimal strings (not hexadecimal literals) to the web3.js APIs. The input for the Solidity address type should also be in hexadecimal strings.
- `web3.eth.getTransactionReceipt()`: This is used to get details about a transaction using its hash. It returns a transaction receipt object if the transaction was found in the blockchain; otherwise, it returns `null`. The transaction receipt object contains the following properties:
  - `blockHash`: The hash of the block where this transaction was located.
  - `blockNumber`: The block number where this transaction was located.
  - `transactionHash`: The hash of the transaction.
  - `transactionIndex`: The integer of the transactions' index position in the block.
  - `from`: The address of the sender.
  - `to`: The address of the receiver; this is left as `null` when it's a contract creation transaction.
  - `cumulativeGasUsed`: The total amount of gas used when this transaction was executed in the block.

- `gasUsed`: The amount of gas used by this specific transaction alone.
- `contractAddress`: The contract address created if the transaction was a contract creation. Otherwise, this is left as `null`.
- `logs`: The array of log objects that this transaction generated.

Sending ether

Let's look at how to send `ether` to any address. To send `ether`, you need to use the `web3.eth.sendTransaction()` method. This method can be used to send any kind of transaction but is mostly used to send `ether`. This is because deploying a contract or calling a method of contract using this method is cumbersome as it requires you to manually generate the data of the transaction rather than automatically generating it. It takes a transaction object that has the following properties:

- `from`: The address for the sending account. This uses the `web3.eth.defaultAccount` property if not specified.
- `to`: This is optional. It's the destination address of the message and is left undefined for a contract-creation transaction.
- `value`: This is optional. The value of the transaction is transferred in wei as well as the endowment if it's a contract-creation transaction.
- `gas`: This is optional. It's the amount of gas to use for the transaction (unused gas is refunded). If this is not provided, then it's automatically determined.
- `gasPrice`: This is optional. It's the price of gas for this transaction in wei, and it defaults to the mean network gas price.
- `data`: This is optional. It's either a byte string containing the associated data of the message or, in the case of a contract-creation transaction, the initialization code.
- `nonce`: This is optional. It's an integer. Every transaction has `nonce` associated with it. `nonce` is a counter that indicates the number of transactions made by the sender. If it is not provided, it will be automatically determined. It helps prevent replay attacks. This `nonce` is not the `nonce` associated with a block. If we are using a `nonce` greater than the `nonce` that the transaction should have, then the transaction is put in a queue until the other transactions arrive. For example, if `nonce` of the next transaction should be four and we set the `nonce` to ten, then geth will wait for the remaining six transactions before broadcasting this transaction. The transaction with `nonce` ten is called a **queued transaction**, and is not a pending transaction.

Here's an example of how to send `ether` to an address:

```
var txnHash = web3.eth.sendTransaction({
  from: web3.eth.accounts[0],
  to: web3.eth.accounts[1],
  value: web3.toWei("1", "ether")
});
```

Here, we send one `ether` from account number 0 to account number 1. We need to make sure that both the accounts are unlocked using the `unlock` option while running geth. The geth interactive console prompts for passwords, but the web3.js API outside of the interactive console will throw an error if the account is locked. This method returns the transaction hash of the transaction. You can then check whether the transaction is mined or not using the `getTransactionReceipt()` method.

You can also use `web3.personal.listAccounts()`, `web3.personal.unlockAccount(addr, pwd)`, and `web3.personal.newAccount(pwd)` APIs to manage accounts at runtime.

Working with contracts

Let's learn how to deploy a new contract, get a reference to a deployed contract using its address, send `ether` to a contract, send a transaction to invoke a `contract` method, and estimate the gas of a method call.

To deploy a new contract or to get a reference to an already deployed contract, you need to first create a `contract` object using the `web3.eth.contract()` method. It takes the contract ABI as an argument and returns the `contract` object.

Here is the code to create a `contract` object:

```
var proofContract = web3.eth.contract([{"constant":false,"inputs":
  [{"name":"fileHash","type":"string"}],"name":"get","outputs":
  [{"name":"timestamp","type":"uint256"},
  {"name":"owner","type":"string"}],"payable":false,"type":"function"},
  {"constant":false,"inputs":[{"name":"owner","type":"string"},
  {"name":"fileHash","type":"string"}],"name":"set","outputs":
  [],"payable":false,"type":"function"},{"anonymous":false,"inputs":
  [{"indexed":false,"name":"status","type":"bool"},
  {"indexed":false,"name":"timestamp","type":"uint256"},
  {"indexed":false,"name":"owner","type":"string"},
  {"indexed":false,"name":"fileHash","type":"string"}],"name"
  :"logFileAddedStatus","type":"event"}]);
```

Once you have the contract, you can deploy it using the `new` method of the `contract` object or get a reference to an already deployed contract that matches the ABI using the `at` method.

Let's take a look at an example of how to deploy a new contract, as follows:

```
var proof = proofContract.new({
      from: web3.eth.accounts[0],
      data: "0x606060405261068...",
      gas: "4700000"
   },
   function(e, contract) {
      if (e) {
         console.log("Error " + e);
      } else if (contract.address != undefined) {
         console.log("Contract Address: " + contract.address);
      } else {
         console.log("Txn Hash: " + contract.transactionHash)
      }
   })
```

Here, the `new` method is called asynchronously, so the callback is fired twice if the transaction was created and broadcasted successfully. On the first occasion, it's called after the transaction is broadcasted, and on the second occasion, it's called after the transaction is mined. If you don't provide a callback, then the `proof` variable will have the `address` property set to `undefined`. Once `contract` is mined, the `address` property will be set.

In the `proof` contract, there is no constructor, but if there is one, then the arguments for the constructor should be placed at the beginning of the `new` method. The object we passed contains the `from` address, the bytecode of the contract, and the maximum `gas` to use. These three properties must be present for the transaction to be created. This object can have the properties that are present in the object passed to the `sendTransaction()` method, but here, `data` is the contract bytecode and the `to` property is ignored.

You can use the `at` method to get a reference to an already deployed contract. Here is the code to demonstrate this:

```
var proof =
   proofContract.at("0xd45e541ca2622386cd820d1d3be74a86531c14a1");
```

Now let's take a look at sending a transaction to invoke a method of a contract. Here is an example to demonstrate this:

```
proof.set.sendTransaction("Owner Name",
    "e3b0c44298fc1c149afbf4c8996fb92427ae41e4649b934ca495991b7852b855", {

from: web3.eth.accounts[0],
}, function(error, transactionHash){

if (!err)

console.log(transactionHash);
})
```

Here, we call the `sendTransaction` method of the object for the namesake method. The object passed to this `sendTransaction` method has the same properties as `web3.eth.sendTransaction()`, except that the `data` and `to` properties are ignored.

If you want to invoke a method on the node itself, rather than creating a transaction and broadcasting it, then you can use `call` instead of `sendTransaction`. Here's how:

```
var returnValue = proof.get.call
    ("e3b0c44298fc1c149afbf4c8996fb92427ae41e4649b934ca495991b7852b855");
```

Sometimes, it is necessary to find out the amount of gas that would be required to invoke a method so that you can decide whether to invoke it. You can use `web3.eth.estimateGas` for this purpose. However, using `web3.eth.estimateGas()` requires you to directly generate the data of the transaction; therefore, we can use the `estimateGas()` method of the contract object. Here is an example to demonstrate this:

```
var estimatedGas = proof.get.estimateGas
    ("e3b0c44298fc1c149afbf4c8996fb92427ae41e4649b934ca495991b7852b855");
```

> To send some `ether` to a contract without invoking any method, you can simply use the `web3.eth.sendTransaction` method.

Retrieving and listening to contract events

Watching for events is very important because the results of method invocations by transactions are usually returned by triggering events.

Before we get into how to retrieve and watch for events, we need to learn about indexed parameters of events. A maximum of three parameters for an event can have the `indexed` attribute. This attribute is used to signal the node to index it so that the app client can search for events with matching return values. If you don't use the `indexed` attribute, then it will have to retrieve all the events from the node and filter the ones needed. For example, you can write the `logFileAddedStatus` event this way:

```
event logFileAddedStatus(bool indexed status, uint indexed timestamp,
  string owner, string indexed fileHash);
```

Here is an example to demonstrate how to listen to contract events:

```
var event = proof.logFileAddedStatus(null, {
 fromBlock: 0,
 toBlock: "latest"
});
event.get(function(error, result) {
 if (!error) {
 console.log(result);
 } else {
 console.log(error);
 }
})
event.watch(function(error, result) {
 if (!error) {
 console.log(result.args.status);
 } else {
 console.log(error);
 }
})
setTimeout(function() {
 event.stopWatching();
}, 60000)
var events = proof.allEvents({
 fromBlock: 0,
 toBlock: "latest"
});
events.get(function(error, result) {
 if (!error) {
 console.log(result);
 } else {
 console.log(error);
 }
})
events.watch(function(error, result) {
 if (!error) {
```

```
  console.log(result.args.status);
  } else {
  console.log(error);
  }
})
setTimeout(function() {
 events.stopWatching();
}, 60000)
```

And the following is how the aforementioned code works:

- First, we get the `event` object by calling the method of the event namesake on a contract instance. This method takes two objects as arguments, which are used to filter events:
  - The first object is used to filter events by indexed return values, for example, `{'valueA': 1, 'valueB': [myFirstAddress, mySecondAddress]}`. All filter values are set to `null` by default. This means that they will match any event of a given type sent from this contract.
  - The next object can contain three properties: `fromBlock` (the `"earliest"` block; by default, it is `"latest"`); `toBlock` (the `"latest"` block; by default, it is `"latest"`); and `address` (a list of addresses to only get logs from; by default, the contract address).
- The `event` object exposes three methods: `get`, `watch`, and `stopWatching`. `get` is used to get all the events in the block range. `watch` is similar to `get`, but it watches for changes after getting the events. `stopWatching` can be used to stop watching for changes.
- Then, we have the `allEvents` method of the contract instance. It is used to retrieve all the events of a contract.

Every event is represented by an object that contains the following properties:

- `args`: An object with the arguments from the event.
- `event`: A string representing the event name.
- `logIndex`: An integer representing the log index position in the block.
- `transactionIndex`: An integer representing the transactions that the index position log was created from.
- `transactionHash`: A string representing the hash of the transactions that this log was created from.
- `address`: A string representing the address from which this log originated.

- `blockHash`: A string representing the hash of the block where this log was located. This is left as `null` when it's pending.
- `blockNumber`: The block number this log was in. This is entered as `null` when it's pending.

> web3.js provides a `web3.eth.filter` API to retrieve and watch for events. You can use this API, but the way of handling events in the earlier method is much easier. You can learn more about it at `https://github.com/ethereum/wiki/wiki/JavaScript-API#web3ethfilter`.

Building a client for the ownership contract

In the previous chapter, we wrote Solidity code for the ownership contract. And in both the previous chapter and this one, we learned about web3.js and how to invoke the methods of the contract using web3.js. Now, it's time to build a client for our smart contract so that users can use it easily.

We will build a client where an enterprise's user selects a file, enters owner details, and then clicks on `Submit` to broadcast a transaction to invoke the contract's `set` method with the file hash and the owner's details. Once the transaction is successfully broadcasted, we will display the transaction hash. The user will also be able to select a file and get the owner's details from the smart contract. The client will also display the recent `set` transactions mined in real time.

We will use sha1.js to get the hash of the file on the frontend, jQuery for DOM manipulation, and Bootstrap 4 to create a responsive layout. We will use Express.js and web3.js on the backend. We will use `socket.io` so that the backend pushes recently mined transactions to the frontend without the frontend periodically requesting data.

The project structure

In the exercise files for this chapter, you will find two directories: `Final` and `Initial`. `Final` contains the final source code of the project, whereas `Initial` contains the empty source code files and libraries to allow you to get started on building the application quickly.

To test the `Final` directory, you will need to run `npm install` inside it and replace the hardcoded contract address in `app.js` with the contract address that you got after deploying the contract. Then, run the app using the `node app.js` command inside the `Final` directory.

In the `Initial` directory, you will find a `public` directory and two files named `app.js` and `package.json`. `package.json` contains the backend dependencies of our app, and `app.js` is where you will place the backend source code.

The `public` directory contains files related to the frontend. Inside `public/css`, you will find `bootstrap.min.css`, which is the Bootstrap library; inside `public/html`, you will find `index.html`, where you will place the HTML code of our app; and in the `public/js` directory, you will find JS files for jQuery, sha1, and socket.io. Inside `public/js`, you will also find a `main.js` file, where you will place the frontend JS code of our app.

Building the backend

First, run `npm install` inside the `Initial` directory to install the required dependencies for our backend. Before we get into coding the backend, make sure geth is running with `rpc` enabled. Finally, make sure that account 0 exists and is unlocked.

One final thing you need to do before getting started with coding is to deploy the ownership contract using the code we saw in the previous chapter, and copy the contract address.

Now let's create a single server, which will serve the HTML to the browser and also accept `socket.io` connections:

```
var express = require("express");
var app = express();
var server = require("http").createServer(app);
var io = require("socket.io")(server);
server.listen(8080);
```

Here, we are integrating both the `express` and `socket.io` servers into one server running on port 8080.

Now let's create the routes to serve the static files and also the home page of the app. Here is the code to do this:

```
app.use(express.static("public"));
app.get("/", function(req, res){
```

```
        res.sendFile(__dirname + "/public/html/index.html");
    })
```

Here, we are using the `express.static` middleware to serve static files. We are asking it to find static files in the `public` directory.

Now let's connect to the geth node and also get a reference to the deployed contract so that we can send transactions and watch for events. Here is the code to do this:

```
var Web3 = require("web3");

web3 = new Web3(new Web3.providers.HttpProvider("http://localhost:8545"));

var proofContract =
web3.eth.contract([{"constant":false,"inputs":[{"name":"fileHash","type":"s
tring"}],"name":"get","outputs":[{"name":"timestamp","type":"uint256"},{"na
me":"owner","type":"string"}],"payable":false,"type":"function"},{"constant
":false,"inputs":[{"name":"owner","type":"string"},{"name":"fileHash","type
":"string"}],"name":"set","outputs":[],"payable":false,"type":"function"},{
"anonymous":false,"inputs":[{"indexed":false,"name":"status","type":"bool"}
,{"indexed":false,"name":"timestamp","type":"uint256"},{"indexed":false,"na
me":"owner","type":"string"},{"indexed":false,"name":"fileHash","type":"str
ing"}],"name":"logFileAddedStatus","type":"event"}]);

var proof =
    proofContract.at("0xf7f02f65d5cd874d180c3575cb8813a9e7736066");
```

The code is self-explanatory. Simply replace the contract address with the one that you got.

Now let's create routes to broadcast transactions and get information about a file. Here is the code to do this:

```
app.get("/submit", function(req, res){
    var fileHash = req.query.hash;
    var owner = req.query.owner;
    var pkeys = req.query.pkeys;

    pkeys = pkeys.split(",")

    proof.set.sendTransaction(owner, fileHash, {
        from: web3.eth.accounts[0],
        privateFor: pkeys
    }, function(error, transactionHash){
        if (!error)
        {
            res.send(transactionHash);
        }
        else
```

```
        {
            res.send("Error");
        }
    })
})

app.get("/getInfo", function(req, res) {
    var fileHash = req.query.hash;
    var details = proof.get.call(fileHash);
    res.send(details);
})
```

Here, the /submit route is used to create and broadcast transactions. Once we get the transaction hash, we send it to the client. We are not doing anything to wait for the transaction to mine. The /getInfo route calls the get method of the contract on the node itself, instead of creating a transaction. It simply sends back whatever response it gets.

Now let's watch for the events from the contract and broadcast them to all the clients. Here is the code to do this:

```
proof.logFileAddedStatus().watch(function(error, result) {
    if (!error) {
        if (result.args.status == true) {
            io.send(result);
        }
    }
})
```

Here, we check whether status is true, and only if it is true do we broadcast the event to all the connected socket.io clients.

Building the frontend

Let's begin with the HTML of the app. Put this code in the index.html file, as follows:

```
<!DOCTYPE html>
<html lang="en">
    <head>
        <meta name="viewport" content="width=device-width, initial-
            scale=1, shrink-to-fit=no">
        <link rel="stylesheet" href="/css/bootstrap.min.css">
    </head>
    <body>
        <div class="container">
            <div class="row">
```

```html
<div class="col-md-6 offset-md-3 text-xs-center">
    <br>
    <h3>Upload any file</h3>
    <br>
    <div>
        <div class="form-group">
            <label class="custom-file text-xs-left">
                <input type="file" id="file"
                  class="custom-file-input">
                <span class="custom-file-control">
                </span>
            </label>
        </div>
        <div class="form-group">
            <label for="owner">Enter owner name</label>
            <input type="text" class="form-control"
               id="owner">
        </div>
        <div class="form-group">
            <label for="owner">Enter Public Keys
            <small>(comma Seperated)</small></label>
            <input type="text" class="form-control"
               id="pkeys">
        </div>
        <button onclick="submit()" class="btn btn-
          primary">Submit</button>
        <button onclick="getInfo()" class="btn btn-
          primary">Get Info</button>
        <br><br>
        <div class="alert alert-info" role="alert"
           id="message">
            You can either submit the file's details or
            get information about it.
        </div>
    </div>
</div>
</div>
<div class="row">
    <div class="col-md-6 offset-md-3 text-xs-center">
        <br>
        <h3>Live Transactions Mined</h3>
        <br>
        <ol id="events_list">No Transaction Found</ol>
    </div>
</div>
</div>
<script type="text/javascript" src="/js/sha1.min.js"></script>
<script type="text/javascript" src="/js/jquery.min.js">
```

```
            </script>
        <script type="text/javascript" src="/js/socket.io.min.js">
            </script>
        <script type="text/javascript" src="/js/main.js"></script>
    </body>
</html>
```

Here is how the code works:

- First, we display Bootstrap's file input field so that the user can select a file.
- Then, we display a text field where the user can enter the owner's details.
- Then we have two buttons. The first one is to store the file hash and the owner's details in the contract, and the second button is to get information on the file from the contract. Clicking on the Submit button triggers the submit() method, and clicking on the Get Info button triggers the getInfo() method.
- Next, we have an alert box to display messages.
- Finally, we display an ordered list to show the transactions of the contract that gets mined while the user is on the page.

Now, let's write the implementation for the getInfo() and submit() methods, establish socket.io connect with the server, and listen for socket.io messages from the server. Place this code in the main.js file:

```
function submit()
{
  var file = document.getElementById("file").files[0];

  if(file)
  {
    var owner = document.getElementById("owner").value;

    if(owner == "")
    {
      alert("Please enter owner name");
    }
    else
    {
      var publicKeys = document.getElementById("pkeys").value;

      if(publicKeys == "")
      {
        alert("Please enter the other enterprise's public keys");
      }
      else
      {
```

```
            var reader = new FileReader();
            reader.onload = function (event) {
                var hash = sha1(event.target.result);

                $.get("/submit?hash=" + hash + "&owner=" + owner +
                "&pkeys=" + encodeURIComponent(publicKeys), function(data){
                  if(data == "Error")
                  {
                    $("#message").text("An error occured.");
                  }
                  else
                  {
                    $("#message").html("Transaction hash: " + data);
                  }
                });
            };
            reader.readAsArrayBuffer(file);
        }
      }
   }
   else
   {
      alert("Please select a file");
   }
}

function getInfo()
{
   var file = document.getElementById("file").files[0];

   if(file)
   {
      var reader = new FileReader();
      reader.onload = function (event) {
          var hash = sha1(event.target.result);

          $.get("/getInfo?hash=" + hash, function(data){
            if(data[0] == 0 && data[1] == "")
            {
              $("#message").html("File not found");
            }
            else
            {
              $("#message").html("Timestamp: " + data[0] + " Owner: " +
                data[1]);
            }
          });
      };
```

```
      reader.readAsArrayBuffer(file);
   }
   else
   {
     alert("Please select a file");
   }
 }

 var socket = io("http://localhost:8080");

 socket.on("connect", function () {
   socket.on("message", function (msg) {
     if($("#events_list").text() == "No Transaction Found")
     {
       $("#events_list").html("<li>Txn Hash: " + msg.transactionHash +
         "\nOwner: " + msg.args.owner + "\nFile Hash: " +
           msg.args.fileHash + "</li>");
     }
     else
     {
       $("#events_list").prepend("<li>Txn Hash: " + msg.transactionHash
         + "\nOwner: " + msg.args.owner + "\nFile Hash: " +
           msg.args.fileHash + "</li>");
     }
   });
 });
```

This is how the preceding code works:

- First, we define the submit() method. In the submit() method, we ensure that a file is selected and the text field is not empty. Then, we read the content of the file as an array buffer and pass the array buffer to the sha1() method exposed by sha1.js in order to get the hash of the content inside the array buffer. Once we have the hash, we use jQuery to make an AJAX request to the /submit route and then we display the transaction hash in the alert box.

- We define the getInfo() method next. It first makes sure that a file is selected. Then, it generates a hash like the one it generated earlier and makes a request to the /getInfo endpoint to get information about that file.

- Finally, we establish a socket.io connection using the io() method exposed by the socket.io library. Then, we wait for the connect event to trigger, which indicates that a connection has been established. After the connection is established, we listen for messages from the server and display the details of the transactions to the user.

We aren't storing the file in the Ethereum blockchain. Storing files is very expensive, as it requires a lot of gas. In our case, we don't need to store files because nodes in the network will be able to see the file; therefore, if the users want to keep the file content secret, then they won't be able to. Our application's purpose is simply to prove ownership of a file, not to store and serve the file, as a cloud service does.

Testing the client

Now run the `app.js` node to run the application server. Open your favorite browser and visit `http://localhost:8080/`. You will see this output in the browser:

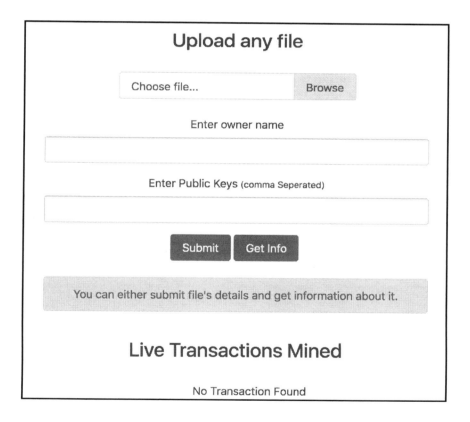

Now select a file, enter the owner's name, and click on **Submit**. The browser window will change to this:

In the following diagram, you can see that the **Transaction hash** is displayed. Now wait until the transaction is mined. Once the transaction is mined, you will be able to see the transaction in the live transactions list. Here is how the browser window should look:

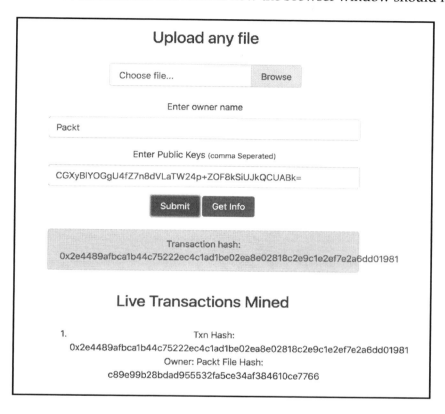

Now select the same file again and click on the **Get Info** button. You will see the following output:

In the previous screenshot, you can see the **Timestamp** and the owner's details. Now we have finished building the client for our first DApp.

Summary

In this chapter, we first learned about the fundamentals of web3.js and looked at some examples. We learned about connecting to a node, basic APIs, sending various kinds of transactions, and watching for events. Finally, we built a proper production use client for our ownership contract. Now you should be comfortable with writing smart contracts and building UI clients for them in order to ease their use.

In the next chapter, we will learn about achieving privacy using a zero-knowledge security layer.

5

Building Interoperable Blockchains

There are various permissioned and public blockchains representing different assets, information, and business processes. One of the major requirements for using these networks is to enable them to talk to each other, which is a major challenge to overcome. It would be great if there were only one blockchain to rule them all, but that's definitely not going to happen, because it's not possible for only one blockchain to win in terms of security, privacy, efficiency, flexibility, platform complexity, developer ease of use, and so on. The future of blockchains will be several public and permissioned blockchains interoperating with each other. In this chapter, we are going to explore how to achieve interoperability between multiple Quorum networks.

In this chapter, we will cover the following topics:

- Understanding what blockchain interoperability means and the various popular projects related to it
- Examining the use cases that interoperable blockchains can achieve
- Looking at the various technologies and patterns that can be used to achieve blockchain interoperability
- Building an interoperable blockchain network representing **FedCoins**

Understanding blockchain interoperability

Interoperable blockchains are blockchains that can talk to each other. Each blockchain can read the other's state. There will be many occasions when you will want to enable your smart contracts to talk to centralized or other decentralized apps. When we talk about interoperability between DApps we're talking about something different than interoperability between blockchains.

Enabling an Ethereum smart contract to check whether a file exists in IPFS or not is enabling interoperability between DApps, whereas enabling an Ethereum smart contract to fetch a Bitcoin account balance is enabling interoperability between blockchains.

Getting Ethereum smart contracts to make REST APIs call to centralized apps is considered enabling interoperability between Ethereum and WWW. But in this chapter, we will learn about interoperability between blockchains, specifically interoperability between Quorum networks.

There are various popular projects being developed that aim to employ decentralized mechanisms to achieve interoperability between blockchains. Various popular projects, such as **Cosmos, Polkadot, Interledger, Block Collider**, and so on, are being actively developed to make blockchain interoperability decentralized and easy to achieve, but in this chapter we won't cover these, as they aim to bring interoperability to public blockchains. However, the strategies that we will learn to create interoperable blockchains are being used by these projects.

What can interoperable blockchains achieve?

Before going further and looking at how to achieve blockchain interoperability, we need to know what kinds of things that interoperable blockchains can achieve. There are obviously many use cases for interoperable blockchains, but we will be looking at the use cases that interoperability between blockchains mostly aims to achieve. It may achieve one or more of the following use cases:

- **Portable assets**: Moving assets back and forth from one blockchain to another. These are also called **one-to-one pegs** or **two-way pegs**.
- **Payment-versus-payment and payment-versus-delivery**: These are technically known as **atomic swaps**. When two users are exchanging assets that reside in two different blockchains, a guarantee is needed, stating that either both transfers happen or neither does. For example, if one blockchain holds digitalized USD and the other holds digitalized EUR, then users should be able to exchange these assets atomically.

- **Fetching information and reacting to events**: One blockchain is able to read information that exists on another blockchain or is able to react to transactions happening on another blockchain. For example, this could be a case where one blockchain represents tenancy contracts and other one represents locked security deposits, so when the tenancy contract expires in the first blockchain, the second one should automatically release the security deposits.

Strategies for implementing blockchain interoperability

Let's look at the various strategies with which you can achieve one or more of the previous use cases. We will learn the strategies that we can implement in Quorum, but not all the ones that are available for public or other blockchains. We will also look at examples of how to implement these strategies.

Single custodian

The easiest way to achieve interoperability is to have a centralized third-party through which blockchains can talk to each other. Essentially, you need to trust the third-party.

However, centralized interoperability projects, such as **Oraclize**, have solved the trust problem. Oraclize enables your Ethereum smart contracts to communicate with the WWW; that is, it enables you to make REST API calls, fetch a Bitcoin account balance, check the file status in IPFS, and so on. Oraclize also provides a proof for smart contracts stating that the results have not been manipulated; therefore, Oraclize has tackled the trust issue, but the single point of failure still remains. Oraclize is available for both permissioned and public Ethereum. Oraclize's major achievement was providing the ability for Ethereum smart contracts to make REST API calls, but its purpose was never to provide interoperability between blockchains, and therefore it doesn't offer this feature.

If trust is not an issue for you, then the single custodian strategy is definitely something you should consider, as this supports all the three use cases we discussed earlier. You can easily write a centralized application that reacts to events on one blockchain and calls actions on another blockchain. In permissioned blockchains, there are usually regulators or authorities that you can choose to host that centralized application. The single custodian should send transactions that are signed using a private key that the blockchains have been pre-programmed to trust.

Multisignature federation

A better option to implement interoperability between blockchains is to have a group of notaries (or authorities) in control of a multisignature, where the majority of them have to approve an action for it to proceed. This setup is better than having a single custodian, but still centralizes control. To achieve true decentralization, the notaries should be carefully selected to have at least the following properties:

- The number of notaries should not be low—for example, at least 10.
- The number of notaries should not be too high—for example, less than 30, so that users can verify the authenticity and honesty of the notaries.
- Notaries should be distributed across different legal jurisdictions and nations to prevent state attacks, coercion, and censorship.
- Notaries should be geographically distributed to prevent failure of the infrastructure in case of natural disasters.
- Notaries should be renown.
- Notaries should not be controlled by (or dependent on) a lower number of entities. For example, notaries cannot be different branches of the same bank.
- Notaries should be able to achieve and maintain a specified level of security through physical and logical protections, together with the required security procedures.

Sidechains or relays

A sidechain is a system inside one blockchain that can validate and read events and/or states in other blockchains. Relays are a more direct method for facilitating interoperability, where instead of relying on trusted intermediaries to provide information about one blockchain to another, the blockchains effectively take on the task of doing that themselves. Currently, sidechain systems are achieved using **Merkle trees**.

The general approach is as follows. Suppose that a smart contract executing on blockchain *B* wants to learn either whether a particular event took place on blockchain *A*, or some particular object in the state of blockchain *A* contained some value at some particular time. We can create a contract on blockchain *B* that takes one of these block headers of blockchain *A* and uses the standard verification procedure for the blockchain *A* consensus algorithm to verify this block header—in IBFT, this would involve verifying that more than 75% of the validators' signatures have signed the block header. Once the relay has verified that the block header has been finalized, the relay can then verify any desired transaction or account/state entry separately by verifying a single branch of the Merkle tree against the block header.

The use of this so-called **light client verification** technology is ideal for relays because of how fundamentally resource constrained a blockchain is. In fact, it is impossible for a mechanism inside blockchain *A* to fully validate blockchain *B* and for a mechanism inside blockchain *B* to fully validate blockchain *A* at the same time, for the same simple mathematical reason that two boxes cannot simultaneously contain each other: *A* would need to rerun the part of *B* that reruns *A*, including the part of *A* that reruns *B*, and so forth. With light client verification, however, a protocol where blockchain *A* contains small pieces of blockchain *B* and blockchain *B* contains small pieces of blockchain *A* that are pulled on-demand is entirely feasible. A smart contract on a relay on blockchain *B* that wants to verify a particular transaction, event, or piece of state information on blockchain *A* would, much like a traditional light client, verify a branch of the cryptographic hash tree of blockchain *A*, then verify with the block header that the root of this branch is inside, and if both checks pass, it would accept that the transaction, event, or state information is correct.

Note that because blockchains are fully self-contained environments and have no natural access to the outside world, the relevant bits of chain *A* would need to be fed into chain *B* by a user; however, because the data is, in a cryptographic sense, self-verifying, the user that feeds in this information need not be trusted.

Hash locking

Hash locking is a technique for achieving atomic exchange of assets. It doesn't require any intermediary. This is how hash locking works:

- Suppose that there are two assets called *A* and *B* in two different blockchains. The owner of asset *A* is *X* and the owner of asset *B* is *Y*.
- If they both want to exchange the assets, then first of all, *X* has to generate a secret, *S*, and compute the hash of the secret, which is *H*. After that, *X* shares *H* with *Y*.

- Now, *X* locks asset *A*, stating that if the *S* for *H* is revealed within *N* seconds by *Y*, then ownership of the asset will be transferred to *Y*; otherwise, the asset will be unlocked after *N* seconds.
- Next, *Y* locks asset *B*, stating that if the *S* for *H* is revealed within *N*/2 seconds by *X*, then ownership of the asset will be transferred to *X*; otherwise, the asset will be unlocked after *N*/2 seconds.
- So now, assets *A* and *B* are locked after *N* and *N*/2 seconds respectively. Now, within *N*/2 seconds, *X* reveals *S* to the *B's* blockchain to claim ownership of the asset. Now, *Y* has the equivalent time to learn *S* and reveal *S* to blockchain *A* to claim ownership.

The reason why *X* gets half of the time given to *Y* to claim the funds is that only *X* knows the secret, and after *Y* locks the funds, *X* can wait almost until the end of *N* seconds and claim the asset, which will not give sufficient time for *Y* to claim their funds. Therefore, *X* can succeed in stealing asset *A* and *B*. To avoid this, we are give *Y* *N* seconds and *X* *N*/2 seconds, so that *Y* will have same amount of time as *X* to claim the asset.

The downside of this technique is that if *X* reveals the *S* to blockchain *B* in between the *N*/2 and *N* seconds, then *X* will not be able to claim ownership of *B*, but *Y* will learn about *S* and have time to claim ownership of *A*. However, this would be the fault of *X*, and can be avoided.

Building a FedCoin

FedCoin is a digital currency issued by a central bank and hedged one to one with their fiat currency. Digitalizing fiat currency using blockchain has several benefits, such as enabling easy cross-border payments, saving reconciliation efforts, and so on.

Let's build some digitalized INR and USD on two different blockchain networks. Then, let's create some atomic swap contracts to enable the exchange of these currencies between banks atomically. This use case would require you to create two different Quorum networks using IBFT consensus. In each network there is one authority, which is the central bank, and *N* number of peers, which are other banks. So, you can assume that in the first network, the **Federal Reserve System (FRS)** is the authority and **Bank of America (BOA)** and ICICI banks are the peers. Similarly, in the second network, the **Reserve Bank of India (RBI)** is the authority and BOA and the ICICI bank are the peers.

You don't have to build this network now because when building and testing smart contracts, you can use only one node with four Ethereum account addresses. This would be enough to simulate the whole scenario.

Smart contracts to digitalize fiat currency

Here is a basic smart contract to create a digitalized USD on a blockchain. This smart contract allows us to issue and transfer digitalized currency:

```
pragma solidity ^0.4.19;

contract USD {
    mapping (address => uint) balances;
    mapping (address => mapping (address => uint)) allowed;
    address owner;
    function USD() {
        owner = msg.sender;
    }
    function issueUSD(address to, uint amount) {
        if(msg.sender == owner) {
            balances[to] += amount;
        }
    }
    function transferUSD(address to, uint amount) {
        if(balances[msg.sender] >= amount) {
            balances[msg.sender] -= amount;
            balances[to] += amount;
        }
    }
    function getUSDBalance(address account) view returns
      (uint balance) {
        return balances[account];
    }
    function approve(address spender, uint amount) {
        allowed[spender][msg.sender] = amount;
    }
    function transferUSDFrom(address from, address to, uint amount) {
        if(allowed[msg.sender][from] >= amount && balances[from]
          >= amount) {
            allowed[msg.sender][from] -= amount;
            balances[from] -= amount;
            balances[to] += amount;
        }
    }
}
```

Here is how the preceding code works:

- First, we defined a mapping to store the amount of USD each bank holds. Each bank can have multiple addresses to achieve privacy. These addresses don't have to be banks; they can also be other smart contracts, as every smart contract also has `address`.
- Next, we assumed that the central bank deploys the contracts. Therefore, we defined the central bank as the issuer by assigning its `address` to `owner`.
- Then, we defined the function `issueUSD` with which the central bank can issue USD to other banks.
- Then, we defined another function, named `transferUSD`, with which banks can transfer USD between themselves.
- Next, we had a function for reading the balance of an account.
- Finally, we had two important functions: `approve` and `transferUSDFrom`. The `transferUSDFrom` function allows contracts to send USD on your behalf. In other words, you are providing APIs for other smart contracts on the same blockchain to manage your funds. The `approve` function is used to provide approval for a smart contract to manage your funds. When calling `approve`, you mention how much of your funds that contract can manage.

Here, we are using a built-in modifier called `view`. `view` signifies that the function cannot modify storage, but will read storage (hence viewing). The `view` functions cannot send or receive Ether. Similarly, there is another modifier called `pure`, which signifies that the return value can only be dependent on input parameters—that is, they cannot even read storage and cannot send or receive Ether. You should use these modifiers as they have several benefits—for example, online the Remix IDE looks for these modifiers while generating UI forms for interacting with the contracts.

Now deploy a similar contract to digitalize INR in the second network. Replace USD with INR in the preceding contract and deploy it. It should look like this:

```
pragma solidity ^0.4.19;

contract INR {
    mapping (address => uint) balances;
    mapping (address => mapping (address => uint)) allowed;
    address owner;
    function INR() {
        owner = msg.sender;
    }
```

```
function issueINR(address to, uint amount) {
    if(msg.sender == owner) {
        balances[to] += amount;
    }
}
function transferINR(address to, uint amount) {
    if(balances[msg.sender] >= amount) {
        balances[msg.sender] -= amount;
        balances[to] += amount;
    }
}
function getINRBalance(address account) view returns
  (uint balance) {
    return balances[account];
}
function approve(address spender, uint amount) {
    allowed[spender][msg.sender] = amount;
}
function transferINRFrom(address from, address to, uint amount) {
    if(allowed[msg.sender][from] >= amount && balances[from]
      >= amount) {
        allowed[msg.sender][from] -= amount;
        balances[from] -= amount;
        balances[to] += amount;
    }
}
}
}
```

Atomic swap smart contracts

We have successfully digitalized fiat currencies. Now it's time to implement the atomic swap smart contracts that will provide the hash locking mechanism. We have an atomic swap smart contract deployment in each of the blockchains—that is, the atomic swap smart contract on the first blockchain will lock USD for a certain period of time and expects an Indian bank (here, it's the ICICI bank) to claim it in the defined time period using the secret. Similarly, the atomic swap contract on the second blockchain will lock INR for a certain period of time and expects an American bank (here, it's BOA) to claim it in the defined time period using the secret.

The following is the atomic swap smart contract for locking USD:

```
pragma solidity ^0.4.19;

import "./USD.sol";
```

```
contract AtomicSwap_USD {
    struct AtomicTxn {
        address from;
        address to;
        uint lockPeriod;
        uint amount;
    }
    mapping (bytes32 => AtomicTxn) txns;
    USD USDContract;
    event usdLocked(address to, bytes32 hash, uint expiryTime,
      uint amount);
    event usdUnlocked(bytes32 hash);
    event usdClaimed(string secret, address from, bytes32 hash);
    function AtomicSwap_USD(address usdContractAddress) {
        USDContract = USD(usdContractAddress);
    }
    function lock(address to, bytes32 hash, uint lockExpiryMinutes,
      uint amount) {
        USDContract.transferUSDFrom(msg.sender, address(this), amount);
        txns[hash] = AtomicTxn(msg.sender, to, block.timestamp +
          (lockExpiryMinutes * 60), amount);
        usdLocked(to, hash, block.timestamp + (lockExpiryMinutes * 60),
          amount);
    }
    function unlock(bytes32 hash) {
        if(txns[hash].lockPeriod < block.timestamp) {
            USDContract.transferUSD(txns[hash].from,
              txns[hash].amount);
            usdUnlocked(hash);
        }
    }
    function claim(string secret) {
        bytes32 hash = sha256(secret);
        USDContract.transferUSD(txns[hash].to, txns[hash].amount);
        usdClaimed(secret, txns[hash].from, hash);
    }
    function calculateHash(string secret) returns (bytes32 result) {
        return sha256(secret);
    }
}
```

Here is how the preceding smart contract works:

- At the time of deploying the smart contract, we provide the contract address of the USD contract so that it can call its functions to transfer funds.
- The lock method was used to lock funds using hash. Obviously, before calling the lock method, BOA must approve this atomic swap contract address to be able to access a certain amount of its funds. It takes hash and locks funds for a certain period of time. amount is specified to indicate how much USD to lock and this amount should be less than equal to the approved amount. The to address specifies the Indian bank's address—that is, the ICICI bank. So, when the ICICI bank comes to claim the funds, they go to this address. This function actually transfers funds to its contract address (that is, address(this)) and fires an event so that ICICI bank can see that funds have been locked.
- The unlock method can be used by BOA to unlock the funds after hash has expired, if the funds are not claimed.
- The claim method is used by ICICI bank to claim the funds using the secret.
- Finally, we used the calculateHash method to calculate hash of a secret.

 Here, we are using BOA and ICICI as examples to explain it simply, but the previous smart contracts will work fine with any number of currencies and banks.

Change USD to INR in the preceding contract to provide an atomic swap smart contract for the second blockchain. Here is how the code will look:

```solidity
pragma solidity ^0.4.19;

import "./INR.sol";

contract AtomicSwap_INR {
    struct AtomicTxn {
        address from;
        address to;
        uint lockPeriod;
        uint amount;
    }
    mapping (bytes32 => AtomicTxn) txns;
    INR INRContract;
    event inrLocked(address to, bytes32 hash, uint expiryTime,
      uint amount);
    event inrUnlocked(bytes32 hash);
    event inrClaimed(string secret, address from, bytes32 hash);
```

```
function AtomicSwap_INR(address inrContractAddress) {
    INRContract = INR(inrContractAddress);
}
function lock(address to, bytes32 hash, uint lockExpiryMinutes,
  uint amount) {
    INRContract.transferINRFrom(msg.sender, address(this), amount);
    txns[hash] = AtomicTxn(msg.sender, to, block.timestamp +
      (lockExpiryMinutes * 60), amount);
    inrLocked(to, hash, block.timestamp + (lockExpiryMinutes * 60),
      amount);
}
function unlock(bytes32 hash) {
    if(txns[hash].lockPeriod < block.timestamp) {
        INRContract.transferINR(txns[hash].from,
          txns[hash].amount);
        inrUnlocked(hash);
    }
}
function claim(string secret) {
    bytes32 hash = sha256(secret);
    INRContract.transferINR(txns[hash].to, txns[hash].amount);
    inrClaimed(secret, txns[hash].from, hash);
}
function calculateHash(string secret) returns (bytes32 result) {
    return sha256(secret);
}
}
```

Testing

Now we have the smart contracts ready for conducting atomic swaps between the assets of two different blockchains. Next, let's write some JavaScript code to test the preceding contracts and conduct an atomic exchange. The following code allows you to do this. For testing and simulation purposes, you can run the following code in one single Quorum node with four accounts:

```
var generateSecret = function () {
    return Math.random().toString(36).substr(2, 9);
};

var web3 = new Web3(new
Web3.providers.HttpProvider("http://localhost:8545"));

var RBI_Address = "0x92764a01c43ca175c0d2de145947d6387205c655";
var FRS_Address = "0xbc37e7ba9f099ba8c61532c6fce157072798fe77";
var BOA_Address = "0x104803ea6d8696afa6e7a284a46a1e71553fcf12";
```

```
var ICICI_Address = "0x84d2dab0d783dd84c40d04692e303b19fa49bf47";

var usdContract_ABI = /* Put JSON here */;
var usdContract_Bytecode = "0x606..."
var atomicswapUSD_ABI = /* Put JSON here */;
var atomicswapUSD_Bytecode = "0x606..."
var inrContract_ABI = /* Put JSON here */;
var inrContract_Bytecode = "0x606..."
var atomicswapINR_ABI = /* Put JSON here */;
var atomicswapINR_Bytecode = "0x606..."

var usdContract = web3.eth.contract(usdContract_ABI);
var usd = usdContract.new({
  from: FRS_Address,
   data: usdContract_Bytecode,
   gas: "4700000"
}, function (e, contract){
  if (typeof contract.address !== 'undefined') {
    var usdContractAddress = contract.address;
    var usdContractInstance = usdContract.at(usdContractAddress)
    var atomicswap_usdContract = web3.eth.contract(atomicswapUSD_ABI);
    var atomicswap_usd = atomicswap_usdContract.new(usdContractAddress, {
        from: FRS_Address,
        data: atomicswapUSD_Bytecode,
        gas: "4700000"
    }, function (e, contract){
        if (typeof contract.address !== 'undefined') {
            var atomicSwapUSDAddress = contract.address;
            var atomicSwapUSDContractInstance =
              atomicswap_usdContract.at(atomicSwapUSDAddress);

            var inrContract = web3.eth.contract(inrContract_ABI);
        var inr = inrContract.new({
            from: RBI_Address,
            data: inrContract_Bytecode,
            gas: "4700000"
        }, function (e, contract){
            if(typeof contract.address !== 'undefined') {
                var inrContractAddress = contract.address;
                var inrContractInstance =
                  inrContract.at(inrContractAddress)
            var atomicswap_inrContract =
              web3.eth.contract(atomicswapINR_ABI);
            var atomicswap_inr = atomicswap_inrContract.new(
                inrContractAddress, {
                from: RBI_Address,
                data: atomicswapINR_Bytecode,
                gas: '4700000'
```

```
        }, function (e, contract){
            if (typeof contract.address !== 'undefined') {
                var atomicSwapINRAddress = contract.address;
                var atomicSwapINRContractInstance =
                    atomicswap_inrContract.at(atomicSwapINRAddress);


            }
        })
        }
    })
    }
    })
    }
})
```

First, we deployed the USD contract and then deployed the atomic swap contract for USD by passing the USD contract's address as the parameter. We deployed these contracts as FRS. Then, we deployed the INR contract and then deployed the atomic swap contract for INR by passing the INR contract's address as the parameter. We deployed these contracts as RBI.

Place the following code where continuation is mentioned:

```
//Issue USD
usdContractInstance.issueUSD.sendTransaction(BOA_Address, 1000,
  {from: FRS_Address}, function(e, txnHash){

  //Fetch USD Balance
  console.log("Bank of America's USD Balance is : " +
    usdContractInstance.getUSDBalance.call(BOA_Address).toString())
  //Issue INR
  inrContractInstance.issueINR.sendTransaction(ICICI_Address, 1000,
   {from: RBI_Address}, function(e, txnHash){

   //Fetch INR Balance
   console.log("ICICI Bank's INR Balance is : " +
     inrContractInstance.getINRBalance.call(ICICI_Address).toString())

   //Generate Secret and Hash
   var secret = generateSecret();
   var hash = atomicSwapUSDContractInstance.calculateHash.call(secret,
     {from: BOA_Address});

   //Give Access to Smart Contract
   usdContractInstance.approve.sendTransaction(atomicSwapUSDAddress,
     1000, {from: BOA_Address}, function(e, txnHash){
```

```
//Give Access to Smart Contract
inrContractInstance.approve.sendTransaction(atomicSwapINRAddress,
  1000, {from: ICICI_Address}, function(e, txnHash){

  //Lock 1000 USD for 30 min
  atomicSwapUSDContractInstance.lock.sendTransaction(ICICI_Address,
hash,
  30, 1000, {from: BOA_Address, gas: 4712388}, function(e, txnHash){

    //Fetch USD Balance
    console.log("USD Atomic Exchange Smart Contracts holds : " +
      usdContractInstance.getUSDBalance.call
      (atomicSwapUSDAddress).toString())

    //Lock 1000 INR for 15 min
    atomicSwapINRContractInstance.lock.sendTransaction(BOA_Address,
  hash, 15, 1000, {from: ICICI_Address, gas: 4712388},
  function(e, txnHash){

      //Fetch INR Balance
      console.log("INR Atomic Exchange Smart Contracts holds : "
        + inrContractInstance.getINRBalance.call
        (atomicSwapINRAddress).toString())

      atomicSwapINRContractInstance.claim(secret, {
        from: BOA_Address, gas: 4712388
      }, function(error, txnHash){
        //Fetch INR Balance
        console.log("Bank of America's INR Balance is : " +
          inrContractInstance.getINRBalance.call
          (BOA_Address).toString())

        atomicSwapUSDContractInstance.claim(secret, {
          from: ICICI_Address, gas: 4712388
        }, function(error, txnHash){
          //Fetch USD Balance
          console.log("ICICI Bank's USD Balance is : " +
            usdContractInstance.getUSDBalance.call
            (ICICI_Address).toString())
        })

      })
    })
  })
})
})
})
})
})
```

Here is how the preceding code works:

1. Here the FRS issued USD to BOA and then the RBI issued INR to the ICICI bank.
2. Then, BOA generated a secret. We use a very basic function to generate a secret. Obviously, in real-world scenarios, you should use some sort of hardware-based tool to generate these sorts of secure secrets.
3. Next, we computed the hash of the secret.
4. BOA and the ICICI bank gave the USD atomic swap and INR atomic contracts access to their funds respectively.
5. BOA locked the USD in the USD atomic swap contract for 30 minutes and stated that only the ICICI bank can claim the funds.
6. Likewise, the ICICI bank locked the INR in the INR atomic swap contract for 15 minutes and stated that only BOA can claim the funds.
7. Finally, BOA went ahead and claimed the INR. As soon as ICICI learned about the secret, it went ahead and claimed the USD.

To test the preceding contract, first copy your Ethereum addresses and replace the ones that I have generated in the previous examples. Then make sure you unlock all four of the accounts in your node. Finally, compile the contracts and populate the ABI and Bytecode variables.

Here, we are using a Solidity function to calculate hash, but you can calculate hash using JavaScript. If you want to calculate the sha256 hash, then you can use any JavaScript library, but if you calculate sha3 (that is, keccak256) as Solidity does in JavaScript, then you need to use the web3.utils library, which provides a function called soliditySha3. This function will calculate the sha3 of given input parameters in the same way Solidity would. This means that arguments will be ABI converted and tightly packed before being hashed.

Summary

In this chapter, we looked at the various options for building interoperable blockchains. To summarize, single custodian, multisignature federations, and hash locking are easy to implement, whereas sidechains are complicated and require a lot of engineering. Soon, we will have production-permissioned blockchain platforms that have sidechains support built in.

Finally, we implemented hash locking by simulating two central and commercial banks. You can go ahead and try to build two different networks and attempt to conduct an atomic exchange.

In the next chapter, we will learn how to build a blockchain as a server for Quorum. While building this, we will learn about the concepts of DevOps and cloud computing too.

Building Quorum as a Service Platform

6

As the deployment of containerized applications using **Kubernetes (K8s)** is growing, it's the right time to learn how we can containerize Quorum for deploying to K8s. In this chapter, we will be building a **Platform as a Service (PaaS)** to make it easy to create Quorum networks. We will start with the fundamentals of cloud computing, Docker, and K8s, and end up with a **Quorum as a Service (QaaS)** platform. What we will build in this chapter is a minimalist **Blockchain as a Service (BaaS)**, compared to the ones provided by various cloud platforms such as Azure, AWS, and BlockCluster.

In this chapter, we will cover the following topics:

What is cloud computing?

- Difference between public, private, and hybrid clouds
- Difference between IaaS, PaaS, and SaaS
- What is Docker and the containerization of applications?
- Introduction to microservices architecture
- Understanding fundamentals of K8s and its advantages
- Installing minikube on your local machine
- Deploying a simple Hello World Node.js app in K8s
- Containerizing Quorum for K8s
- Building a QaaS platform using Docker and K8s

Introduction to cloud computing

In simple terms, cloud computing is the on-demand delivery of computing services (servers, storage, databases, networking, software, and more) over the internet.

Cloud computing provides an easier way to access servers, storage, databases, and a broad set of application services over the internet. Cloud services platforms, such as **Amazon Web Services** and **Microsoft Azure**, own and maintain the network-connected hardware required for these application services, while you provision and use what you need by way of a web application.

Here are the advantages of cloud computing:

- **Cost**: Cloud computing saves a lot of cost as you don't have to buy hardware and software. It also saves you the cost of setting up and running on-site data centers. Even if you set up your own data centers, you need IT experts who can manage them, and 24/7 electricity and cooling, which creates additional costs. Compared to this, cloud computing is very cheap. In cloud computing, you can only pay when you consume resources and you only pay for how much you consume.
- **Speed**: Cloud computing saves time as you can get the services running whenever you need; it offers on-demand provisioning of computing services.
- **Scaling globally**: You can easily deploy your applications in multiple regions. This lets you put the applications close to your users.

There are various other benefits, depending on which cloud computing provider you are using.

Private versus public versus hybrid cloud

A cloud solution can be private, public, or hybrid, based on the ownership and location of the data centers. Cloud solutions are usually public, that is, anyone with access to the internet can use the computing services provided by the cloud. All the benefits we saw earlier are benefits provided by public clouds.

Although public clouds let you choose your region while provisioning a computing service, the total number of regions that are available is still very limited. This is a concern for entities such as banks, Armed Forces, and governments as they either don't want the data to leave their country or don't want the cloud provider to have visibility of the data. Therefore, these entities either choose a private or hybrid cloud.

A cloud is said to be private when it is hosted on the enterprise's own data centers. In this case, enterprises don't get the benefits of cost and multi-region scaling as they are responsible for provisioning and maintaining the data centers.

The term hybrid cloud is used when enterprises use a mix of both private and public clouds, based on technical and business requirements. An enterprise may choose to host the application on a public cloud while keeping some data relating to the application in a private cloud due to compliance or security issues.

IaaS versus PaaS and SaaS

Infrastructure as a Service (IaaS), **Platform as a Service (PaaS)**, and **Software as a Service (SaaS)** are three different categories of cloud solutions based on what you manage and what the cloud provider manages for you.

In IaaS, the cloud provider provides customers with on-demand access to basic computing services, that is, storage, networking, and servers. Everything else is up to you to provision and manage. Amazon AWS, Google Cloud, Azure, Linode, and Rackspace are examples of IaaS.

In PaaS, the cloud provider manages the operating system, runtime for programming languages, databases, and web server—that is, it provides an environment for developing, testing, and managing applications. In simple terms, you should only be worried about writing code and the business side of scalability. The rest of the infrastructure for application development and deployment is handled by the cloud provider. Heroku, Redhat's OpenShift, Apache Stratos, and Google App Engine are examples of PaaS.

Database as a Service (DBaaS or **BaaS)** falls under the category of PaaS. So in this chapter, we will be creating a simple PaaS: QaaS. Any cloud solution that manages the services (such as a database, blockchain, or messaging queue) that your applications depends on is PaaS.

In SaaS, the cloud provider manages everything, including the data and the application. You don't write any code to build the application. The cloud provider provide an interface to customize the application based on your needs and deploys it. Use of SaaS tends to reduce the cost of software ownership by removing the need for technical staff to manage, write code, and upgrade software regularly. You just worry about business logic. Salesforce, Google Apps, and WordPress.com are examples of SaaS.

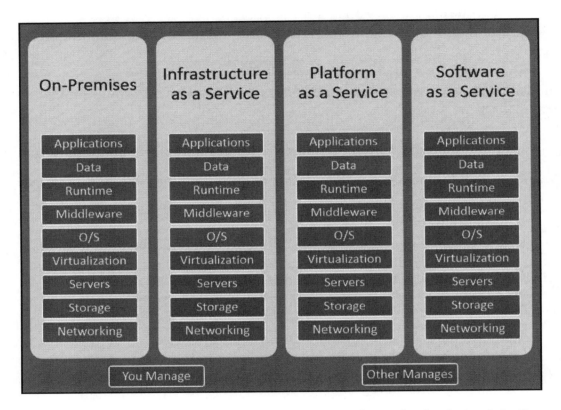

The preceding image can be used to easily determine whether a cloud solution is IaaS, PaaS, or SaaS.

 Some cloud solutions provide features of both IaaS and PaaS. For example, AWS started as an IaaS and now it also provides various on-demand services (such as blockchain and elastic search).

What are containers?

If you are using a PaaS or SaaS to create your application, then you will not come across containers because they take care of containerizing your application. PaaS simply lets you push the source code of your app to the cloud and it builds and runs the app for you.

If you are using IaaS to build your application, then without containerizing your application, it will become next to impossible to scale and manage your application. Let's take a scenario and try to understand why we need containers.

In IaaS, to deploy your app you would need to perform the following steps:

Provision a **Virtual Machines (VMs)**

1. Install all the dependencies and runtime environments of the app
2. Run the app
3. If the app starts receiving more traffic than the VM can handle, you will start creating new VMs and distribute the traffic using a load-balancer
4. For every new VM, you need to follow the same procedure for installing the dependencies and runtime environments before running new instances of the app in the new VMs

This process of rolling up new VMs and running an instance of the app in them is error-prone and time-consuming. This is where containers come in.

In a nutshell, containers are a way of packing an application. What makes containers special is that there are no unexpected errors when you move them to a new machine, or between environments. All of your application's code, libraries, and dependencies are packed together in the container as an immutable artifact. You can think of running a container as running a VM, without the overhead of spinning up an entire operating system. For this reason, bundling your application in a container versus a VM will improve startup time significantly. Containers are much more lightweight and use far fewer resources than VMs.

So, for the preceding example, you would need to create a container for your application and run the container in each of the VMs. Obviously, based on your application architecture, one Docker container can run multiple processes and one VM can run multiple containers.

Internally, PaaS and SaaS use containers to package and deploy your applications. There are many other use cases for containers. For example: a coding test app actually containerizes your code before executing it so that the code executes in an isolated environment.

By containerizing the application and its dependencies, differences in OS distributions and underlying infrastructure are abstracted away. Containers work on bare-metal systems, cloud instances, and VMs across Linux, Windows, and macOS.

Introduction to Docker

Docker helps you create and deploy software within containers. It's an open source collection of tools that help you build, ship, and run any app, anywhere. With Docker, you create a special file called a Dockerfile in your app source code directory. Dockerfiles define a build process, which, when fed to the `docker build` command, will produce an immutable Docker image. You can think of Docker image like a VM image. When you want to start it up, just use the `docker run` command to run it anywhere the Docker daemon is supported and running. A Docker container is a running instance of a Docker image.

In the Dockerfile, you need to mention a command that should be run, then the container starts. This is how the actual application is executed inside the container. If the command exists, the container also shuts down. When a container shuts down, all data written in the container's volume is lost.

Docker also provides a cloud-based repository called **Docker Hub**. You can think of it like a GitHub for Docker images. You can use Docker Hub to create, store, and distribute the container images you build.

Building a Hello World Docker container

Let's create a Docker image that packages a simple Node.js app that exposes an endpoint to print Hello World. Before continuing, make sure you have installed Docker CE (community edition) on your local machine. You can find instructions on install and startingDocker based on different operating systems at `https://docs.docker.com/install/`.

Now create a directory named `hello-world` and create a file named `app.js` in it. Place the following in that file:

```
const http = require('http');

const name = 'node-hello-world';
```

```
const port = '8888';

const app = new http.Server();

app.on('request', (req, res) => {
  res.writeHead(200, { 'Content-Type': 'text/plain' });
  res.write('Hello World');
  res.end('\n');
});

app.listen(port, () => {
  console.log(`${name} is listening on port ${port}`);
});
```

Now create a file named `Dockerfile` in the same directory and place this content in it:

```
FROM node:carbon

WORKDIR /usr/src/app

COPY . ./

EXPOSE 8888

CMD [ "node", "app.js" ]
```

We put the instructions to build the Docker image in the Docker file. You can find the list of instructions at `https://docs.docker.com/engine/reference/builder/`.

Here is how the preceding Dockerfile works:

- First, you need to define from what image we want to build. Here, we will use the latest **long-term support (LTS)** version carbon of node available from the Docker Hub. This image comes with `Node.js` and `npm` already installed.
- Next, we create a directory to hold the application code inside the image; this will be the working directory for your application.
- To bundle your app's source code inside the Docker image, we use the `COPY` instruction. Here it means we are copying from the current host operating system's working directory to Docker's working directory.
- Your app binds to port `8888` so you'll use the `EXPOSE` instruction to have it mapped by the Docker daemon.
- Last but not least, define the command to run your app using `CMD`, which defines your runtime.

Here is how to build the Docker image:

1. Use the `docker build -t nodejs-hello-world .` command to build the Docker image.
2. To run the container, run the `docker run -p 8090:8888 -d nodejs-hello-world` command.
3. The `-p` option binds port `8888` of the container to TCP port `8090` on `127.0.0.1` of the host machine. You can also specify the udp and sctp ports. Visit `http://localhost:8090/` on your web browser and you will see the **Hello World** message.

In Dockerfile, the command is defined using `ENTRYPOINT` and the arguments to the command are defined using `CMD`. The default entry point is `["/bin/sh", "-c']`, which is actually running the `sh` shell. So in the preceding Dockerfile, the main command is starts the `sh` shell and passes the command to run our application as a subcommand. The `-c` option takes a command to run inside the `sh` shell.

Understanding the microservices architecture

The microservices architecture is an application architecture adopted for building enterprise-level applications. To understand microservices architecture, it's important to first understand monolithic architecture, which is its opposite. In monolithic architecture, different functional components of the server-side application, such as payment processing, account management, push notifications, and other components, all blend together in a single unit.

For example, applications are usually divided into three parts. The parts are HTML pages or native UI that run on the user's machine, a server-side application that runs on the server, and a database that also runs on the server. The server-side application is responsible for handling HTTP requests, retrieving and storing data in a database, and executing algorithms. If the server-side application is a single executable (that is, running is a single process) that does all these tasks, then we say that the server-side application is monolithic. This is a common way of building server-side applications. Almost every major CMS, web server, and server-side framework is built using monolithic architecture. This architecture may seem successful, but problems are likely to arise when your application is large and complex.

In microservices architecture, the server-side application is divided into services. A service (or microservice) is a small and independent process that constitutes a particular functionality of the complete server-side application. For example, you can have a service for payment processing, another service for account management, and so on; the services need to communicate with each other by means of a network.

The services can communicate with each other via REST APIs or a messaging queue, depending on whether you need the communication to be synchronous or asynchronous, respectively.

Here are some of the benefits of using microservices architecture:

- As the services communicate by means of a network, they can be written in different programming languages using different frameworks
- Making a change to a service only requires that particular service to be redeployed, instead of all the services, which is a faster procedure
- It becomes easier to measure how many resources are consumed by each service as each service runs in a different process
- It becomes easier to test and debug, as you can analyze each service separately
- Services can be reused by other applications as they interact through network calls
- Small teams work in parallel and can iterate faster than large teams
- Smaller components take up fewer resources and can be scaled to meet increasing demand of that component only

You don't have to run each microservice in a different VM, that is, you can run multiple services in a single VM. The ratio of server to services depends on different factors. A common factor is the amount and type of resources and technologies required. For example, if a service needs a lot of RAM and CPU time, it would be better to run it individually on a server. If there are some services that don't need many resources, you can run them all in a single server together.

Diving into K8s

Once you have created a few Docker containers, you'll realize that something is missing. If you want to run multiple containers across multiple machines – which you'll need to do if you're using microservices—there is still a lot of work to do.

You need to start the right containers at the right time, figure out how they can talk to each other, handle storage considerations, and deal with failed containers or hardware. Doing all of this manually would be a nightmare. Luckily, that's where K8s comes in.

K8sis an open source container-orchestration platform, allowing large numbers of containers to work together in harmony, reducing the operational burden. It helps with things such as:

- Running containers across many different machines.
- Scaling up or down by adding or removing containers when demand changes.
- Keeping storage consistent with multiple instances of an application.
- Distributing load between the containers.
- Launching new containers on different machines if something fails, that is, auto-healing.
- Apps built to work with K8s can easily be moved by one IaaS to another without any changes to the app source code. Apps are deployed on the K8s cluster and the K8s cluster is deployed on IaaS.

From a developer point of view, in a K8s cluster there are two types of machines: master and nodes (also called **worker nodes**). Our application runs on the nodes, whereas the master controls the nodes and exposes the K8s APIs. K8s can be installed on bare metal or on VMs. There are also Kubernetes-as-a-service cloud solutions available, which can create a cluster for you on demand. For example: Google Cloud's Kubernetes Engine, **Azure Kubernetes Service (AKS)**, and **Amazon Elastic Container Service for Kubernetes (Amazon EKS)**.

Getting into resource objects

You can use the K8s API to read, write, and update K8s resource objects by means of a K8s API endpoint. K8s resource objects are entities used to represent the state of the cluster. We need to use manifests to define resource objects. In the API calls, we pass the manifest file contents.

This is a high-level overview of the basic categories of resources provided by the K8s API. Their primary functions are as follows:

- **Workload**: These resources are used to manage and run your containers on the cluster. For example: deployments, pods, job, and replicaset.
- **Discovery and load-balancing**: These resources are used to combine your workloads together into an externally accessible, load-balanced service. For example: service and ingress.
- **Config and storage**: These resources are used to inject initialization data into your applications, and to persist data that is external to your container. For example: config map, secret, and volume.
- **Cluster**: These objects define how the cluster itself is configured; these are typically used only by cluster operators.
- **Metadata**: These resources are used to configure the behavior of other resources within the cluster. For example: network policy and namespaces.

 Dockerfiles let you specify a lot of information regarding how to run the container, such as ports to expose, environmental variables, and which command to run when the container starts. But K8s recommends you move these to the K8s manifest files instead of Dockerfile. Dockerfiles now only specify how to build and package the app. Also, the K8s manifest overwrites instructions in the Dockerfile.

Deployments and pods

K8s encourages you to think of deployment as a representation of a microservice. For example: if you have five microservices, you need to create five deployments, whereas a pod is an instance of a microservice. Suppose you want to run three instances of a microservice and distribute traffic among them, then in your deployment you will define that you need three replicas, which will create three pods. A pod runs one or more containers representing a microservice.

When creating a deployment, you can specify the amount of computing resources the microservice needs, such as memory and CPU, instead of letting it consume everything that's available. You can also specify a node name to run the pod in instead of K8s deciding.

When creating a deployment, you can specify which ports of a Docker container to expose, environment variables, and various other things that are also specified in the Dockerfile.

Services

By default, there is no way deployments can communicate with each other. Services are created to enable communication between microservices and optionally allow microservices to be reached from outside the cluster. We need to create a service for every deployment. Services have a built-in load-balancing feature: if there are three pods of a microservice, then the K8s service automatically distributes traffic between them. Here are the various types of services:

- `ClusterIP`: This is the default service type. Exposes the service on an internal IP in the cluster. This type makes the service only reachable from within the cluster.
- `NodePort`: Makes a service accessible from outside the cluster. It's superset of `ClusterIP`. When we create a service with the `NodePort` type, K8s opens up one or more ports (depending on the number of ports the Docker container exposes) within the `30000-32767` range and maps to container ports in all the worker nodes. So if an instance of the microservice is not running, for example, in machine three still the port is exposed on machine three. K8s handles internal routing. So you can use any of the worker nodes' public IP combined with the assigned port to reach the microservice. If you don't want K8s to pick a random port between `30000-32767` for exposing externally, then you can specify a port between the same range.
- `LoadBalancer`: It's also used to expose a service outside of a cluster. It will spin up a load-balancer in front of the service. This works only on supported cloud platforms, such as AWS, GCP, and Azure.

Ingress controllers and resources

Ingress is a K8s feature used to load-balance and expose microservices outside of the cluster. Compared to NodePort and LoadBalances, it's the feature-rich and recommended way of load-balancing and exposing microservices. Ingress gives you a way to route requests to services based on the request host or path, thus centralizing a number of services into a single entry point, which makes it easier to manage a large application. Ingress also supports SSL offloading, URL rewrites, and many other features so you don't have to integrate all these in each microservice you create.

Ingress is split into two main pieces: ingress controller and resource. Ingress controller is the actual reverse proxy that is exposed outside of the cluster and ingress resources are configurations for the controller. Ingress controller itself is a microservice, that is, it's a deployment and a service is created for it, of type `NodePort` or `LoadBalancer`. The ingress controller has the ability to read the ingress resources and reconfigure itself.

There are various different implementations of ingress controllers available and you should choose the one that best fits your purpose. They vary based on features and the load-balancer and reverse proxy software that they use. K8s official has developed the `NGINX` ingress controller and it's the most common ingress controller for K8s. This ingress controller implementation uses the NGINX reverse proxy and load-balancer.

> You can have a replica of more than one while deploying an ingress controller to get high availability and load-balancing of ingress. You can also have multiple ingresses deployed, which are differentiated using classes.

ConfigMaps and secrets

Almost every application needs some sort of configurations to be passed before running it. For example, when starting a Node.js app, you may need to pass the MongoDB URL as you cannot hardcode it because it differs between development and production environments. These configurations are usually supplied as environment variables or in a configuration file.

K8s lets you specify environment variables in the manifest of a deployment. But if you want to change them, you have to modify the deployment. Even worse, if you want to use the variable with multiple deployments, you have to duplicate the data. K8s provides ConfigMaps (for non-confidential data) and Secrets (for confidential data) to solve this problem.

The big difference between secrets and configmaps is that secrets are obfuscated with a Base64 encoding. Now you can pass configmaps and secrets as environmental variables in a mainfest of deployment. When the configmap or secret changes, the environmental variables also change without any restart or manual activity.

If your application uses configuration files instead of environment variables, they can also be passed using configmaps and secrets.

Bind mounts and volumes

In K8s and Docker, a bind mount is a file or directory on the host machine that is mounted into a container. The file or directory is referenced by its full or relative path on the host machine.

In computer-data storage, a volume is a persistence storage area with a single filesystem, typically (though not necessarily) resident on a single partition of a hard disk. IaaS providers let us create volumes and attach to the VMs. K8s provides features called **persistence volumes** and persistence volume claims, which can automatically create volumes of a specific cloud provider and attach to a pod. Volumes are used when your application needs to save (persist) data. The volumes are made accessible inside the Docker container by bind mounts.

 In K8s, there is a resource object called **StatefulSets**, which is similar to deployments. If your deployment needs persistence storage and you have more than one replica, then you have to create StatefulSets instead of a deployment because deployment cannot assign a separate persistence volume to each pod.

Labels and selectors

Labels are key/value pairs that are attached to resource objects, such as pods, services, and deployments. Labels are intended to specify identifying attributes of objects that are meaningful and relevant to users. Labels can be used to organize and select subsets of objects. Labels can be attached to objects at creation-time and subsequently added and modified at any time. Each object can have a set of key/value labels defined. For example, when creating a service, we specify the list of pods that should be exposed using labels and selectors.

Getting started with minikube

When you are building a real application, the right way to use K8s is to create a development cluster on-premise or on-cloud, depending on whether you will host your app on-premises or on cloud. But to experiment and play around with K8s, you can use minikube.

Minikube is a tool that makes it easy to run K8s locally. Minikube runs a single worker node K8s cluster inside a VM on your laptop for users looking to try out K8s or develop with it day to day. At the time of writing this book, the latest version of minikube is 0.26.1. Minikube can be installed on Windows, macOS, and Ubuntu.

Installing minikube on macOS

First, install a Hypervisor supported by minikube. In macOS, it's recommended to use hyperkit. Install the `hyperkit` driver using the following command:

```
curl -LO
https://storage.googleapis.com/minikube/releases/latest/docker-machine-driv
er-hyperkit \
&& chmod +x docker-machine-driver-hyperkit \
&& sudo mv docker-machine-driver-hyperkit /usr/local/bin/ \
&& sudo chown root:wheel /usr/local/bin/docker-machine-driver-hyperkit \
&& sudo chmod u+s /usr/local/bin/docker-machine-driver-hyperkit
```

Then install `kubectl`. `kubectl` is a command-line tool to deploy and manage applications on K8s. Here is the command to install it:

```
brew install kubectl
```

Now, install minikube using the following command:

```
curl -Lo minikube
https://storage.googleapis.com/minikube/releases/v0.26.1/minikube-darwin-am
d64 && chmod +x minikube && sudo mv minikube /usr/local/bin/
```

Installing minikube on Ubuntu

In Ubuntu, it's recommended to use hyperkit. Install hyperkit using the following command:

```
curl -LO
https://storage.googleapis.com/minikube/releases/latest/docker-machine-driv
er-hyperkit \
&& chmod +x docker-machine-driver-hyperkit \
&& sudo mv docker-machine-driver-hyperkit /usr/local/bin/ \
&& sudo chown root:wheel /usr/local/bin/docker-machine-driver-hyperkit \
&& sudo chmod u+s /usr/local/bin/docker-machine-driver-hyperkit
```

Then install `kubectl`. Here is the command to install it:

```
sudo snap install kubectl --classic
```

Now, install `minikube` using the following command:

```
curl -Lo minikube
https://storage.googleapis.com/minikube/releases/v0.26.1/minikube-linux-amd
64 && chmod +x minikube && sudo mv minikube /usr/local/bin/
```

Installing minikube on Windows

In Windows, it's recommended to use the VirtualBox hypervisor. Download and install VirtualBox from `https://www.virtualbox.org/wiki/Downloads`.

Then download the `kubectl` command from `https://storage.googleapis.com/kubernetes-release/release/v1.10.0/bin/windows/amd64/kubectl.exe`.

Finally, install minikube by downloading and running the minikube installer from `https://github.com/kubernetes/minikube/releases/download/v0.26.1/minikube-installer.exe`.

Starting minikube

On Linux and macOS, start minikube using the following command:

```
minikube start --vm-driver=hyperkit
```

And on Windows, start minikube using the following command:

```
minikube start --vm-driver=virtualbox
```

Change the `--vm-driver` option's value if you are using a different hypervisor. It will take a few minutes to start minikube.

Stopping and deleting minikube

If you want to stop the minikube cluster at any time, you can use the following command:

```
minikube stop
```

You can restart the same cluster using the preceding minikube start commands. If you want to delete the whole cluster, you can use the following command:

```
minukube delete
```

Minikube status

To check the status of minikube, that is, whether the cluster is running or not, you can use the following command:

```
minikube status
```

If it's running successfully, you will see a response similar to this:

```
minikube: Running
cluster: Running
kubectl: Correctly Configured: pointing to minikube-vm at 192.168.64.7
```

Note that here you will see a different IP address. This is the IP address of the minikube VM; that is, the master and worker run inside this VM. Your will access you applications from this IP.

Accessing the K8s dashboard

The K8s dashboard is a general-purpose, web-based UI for K8s clusters. It allows users to manage applications running in the cluster and troubleshoot them, and the cluster itself. To access the dashboard, run this command:

```
minikube dashboard
```

It will open the dashboard in a new browser window. The K8s dashboard will look similar to the following:

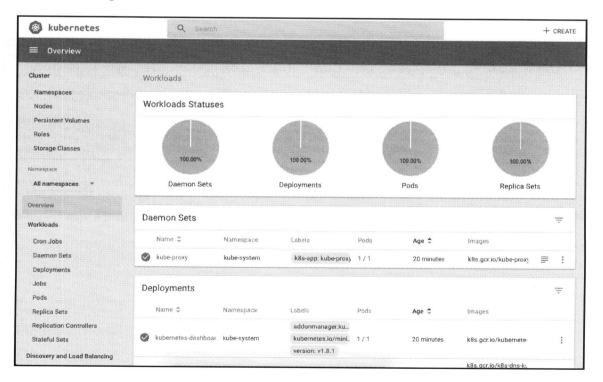

Deploying the Hello World app on k8s

Let's deploy the `Hello World` Docker image we built earlier to the K8s cluster we just created. To create a deployment and service, you need to create a mainfest file with all the details about the deployment and service, and then feed it to K8s using the `kubctl` command. In the mainfest file, you need to provide the remote URL of the Docker image for K8s to pull and run the images. K8s can pull images from the public Docker registry (that is, Docker Hub) or private docker registries.

Pushing images to Docker Hub

Before we push an image, let's understand some basic terminologies related to Docker:

- **Registry**: A service that is storing your Docker images.
- **Repository**: A collection of different Docker images with the same name that have different tags (versions).
- **Tag**: Metadata you can use to distinguish versions of your Docker images so you can preserve older copies. When we created the Docker image earlier, we didn't provide a tag, so the default tag is `latest`. You can create a new tagged image from another image using the `docker tag`
  `[:HOST|:USERID]IMAGE_NAME[:TAG_NAME]`
  `[:HOST|:USERID]IMAGE_NAME[:TAG_NAME]` command. The host prefix is optional and is used to indicate the hostname of the Docker registry if the image belongs to a private Docker registry. If the image is for Docker Hub, then mention the username of your Docker Hub account.

To push an image to Docker Hub, you first need to create a Docker Hub account. Visit `hub.docker.com` and create an account. After you log in, you will see a screen similar to the following:

Now click on **Create Repository** and fill in the following form:

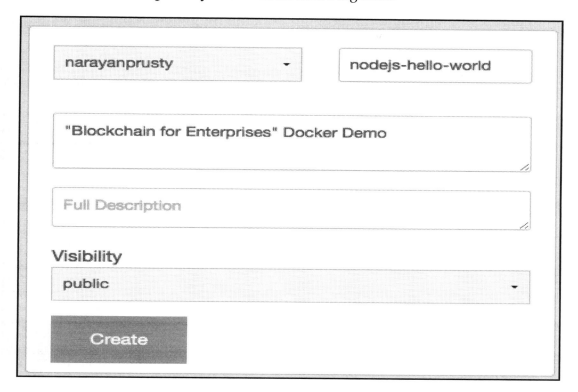

Visibility indicates whether the repository will be private or public. Private repositories aren't visible to everyone. You need to log in to Docker Hub to be able to pull it if you have access to it. You can create only one free private repository on Docker Hub. Once you have created the repository, you will see a screen similar to this:

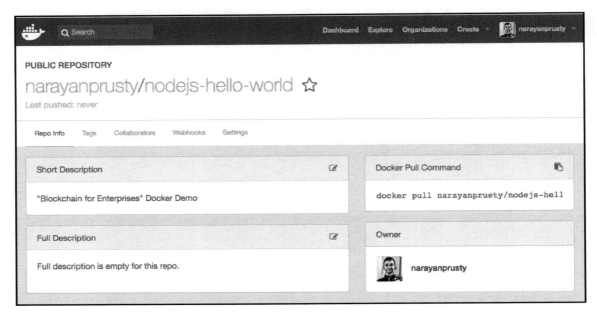

To push the image that you have on your local machine, you need to first log in to Docker Hub from the command line. To do that, run the following command:

```
docker login
```

Then type the username and password of your Docker Hub account when prompted. You should see a login succeeded message. Now tag your image using the following command:

```
docker tag nodejs-hello-world:latest narayanprusty/nodejs-hello-world
```

Now run this command to push the image:

```
docker push narayanprusty/nodejs-hello-world
```

It may take a few minutes to push the depending on your internet bandwidth. Once pushed, click on the **Tags** tab on the repository and you will see a screen similar to this:

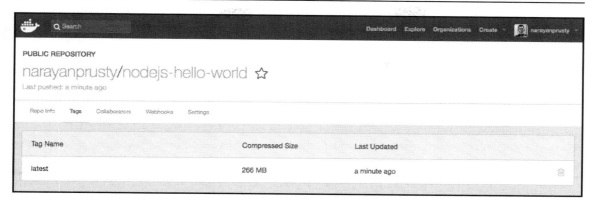

Creating deployments and services

Now, let's create the mainfest file that contains information about the deployment and service. We can create two different or a single deployment file for our deployment and service. Mainfest files can be written in the YAML or JSON format. YAML is preferred, so we will also write in YAML.

Create a file named `helloWorld.yaml` and place the following content in it:

```yaml
apiVersion: apps/v1beta1
kind: Deployment
metadata:
  name: hello-world
spec:
  replicas: 1
  template:
    metadata:
      labels:
        app: hello-world
    spec:
      containers:
      - name: nodejs-hello-world
        image: narayanprusty/nodejs-hello-world
        command: [ 'node', 'app.js']
        workingDir: /usr/src/app
        imagePullPolicy: Always
        ports:
        - containerPort: 8888
---
kind: Service
apiVersion: v1
metadata:
```

```
   name: hello-world
spec:
  ports:
    - name: api
      port: 8888
  selector:
      app: hello-world
  type: NodePort
```

Most of the things in the preceding mainfest file are self-explanatory. Here, you will notice that we have a field called `imagePullPolicy`. The default image pull policy is `IfNotPresent`, which causes the K8s to skip pulling an image if it already exists. If you would like to always force a pull, you can use the `Always` policy, the `:latest` tag, or no tag.

command in K8s is the same as Dockerfile's `ENTRYPOINT`. `arguments` in K8s is the same as `CMD` in Dockerfile. If you do not supply a command or args for a Container, the defaults defined in the Docker image are used. If you supply a command but no `args` for `Container`, only the supplied command is used. The default `ENTRYPOINT` and the default `CMD` defined in the Docker image are ignored. If you supply only args for `Container`, the default `ENTRYPOINT` defined in the Docker image is run with `args` that you supplied. If you supply a command and args, the default `ENTRYPOINT` and the default `CMD` defined in the Docker image are ignored. Your command is run with your args.

Now feed the mainfest to K8s with the following command:

```
kubectl apply -f helloWorld.yaml
```

The `apply` subcommand is used to feed the mainfest file to K8s. If you would like to update a deployment or service configuration, change the file and re-run the command. After the preceding command is executed successfully, open the K8s dashboard and you will see that the deployment and services are created successfully.

Now, to make an HTTP request to the container, we need the worker node IP and port number exposed by the service. Use the `minikube ip` command to find the IP and open the service in the K8s dashboard to find the exposed port number, as shown in the following screenshot:

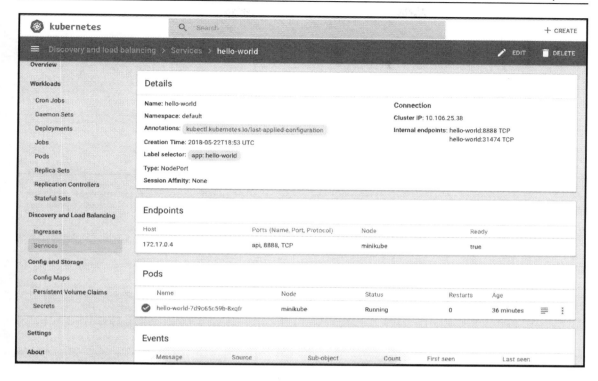

In my case, the port number is `31474`. You will see a different port number. Use the port number and IP to make a request in the browser and you will see the *Hello World* message.

To delete a deployment, use the `kubectl delete deployment deployment_name` command, and to delete a service, use the `kubectl delete svc service_name` command.

Building QaaS

Now let's start building a QaaS platform, this lets us deploy, create, and join networks with just a click of a button. As you are aware, starting a Quorum node requires a lot of manual steps, such as creating the `genesis.json` file, the `static-nodes.json` file, and enode. As we are aiming to automate all these steps, it would require us to write automation scripts to perform these steps. So instead of writing complicated automation scripts, we will use **Quorum Network Manager (QNM)**, which allows users to create and manage Quorum networks easily without any manual steps.

QNM is an open source wrapper for Quorum to make it easy to set up Quorum networks. When you are using QNM, you no longer have to worry about enode, wallets, the genesis file, the static-nodes.json file, and so on. You can find the official QNM repository at `https://github.com/ConsenSys/QuorumNetworkManager`. At the time of writing, the latest version of QNM is `v0.7.5-beta`.

Note that QNM currently works only with Ubuntu 16.04.

In our QaaS, we will deploy Quorum nodes as deployments in K8s. Whenever you want to start a network or join an existing network, a new deployment will be created. QNM is not containerized, so our first step in building QaaS is to containerize it.

How does QNM work?

Before containerising QNM, let's understand how it works. The first step is to install QNM. QNM can be installed in two ways: either by running the install script provided (`setup.sh` file) or manually. We will install it by running the script. The script takes care of installing everything that's needed to use QNM.

You can start a Quorum node with QNM using the `node setupFromConfig.js` command. There are two ways to provide configurations while running a QNM node: using the `config.js` file or using environmental variables. You can also start a node using the `node index.js` command, which will provide an interactive way to configure the node.

In QNM, to create a network, you have to do the following steps:

1. Create a coordinating node
2. Add nodes dynamically to the network

The first node of the network should be the coordinating node; other dynamically-added nodes are non-coordinating nodes. The other-dynamically added nodes connect to the coordinating node to fetch information and configuration related to the network.

The only thing you need to care about is that when starting the first node, you make sure it's a coordinating node. When starting other dynamic nodes, make sure you provide the coordinating node IP address.

The rest of the process is taken care of by the QNM automatically.

Containerizing QNM

Dockerfile to Dockerize QNM will involve installing QNM. Here is the content of the Dockerfile:

```
FROM ubuntu:16.04

#Install Utilities
RUN apt-get update
RUN apt-get install -y --no-install-recommends vim less net-tools
inetutils-ping wget curl git telnet nmap socat dnsutils netcat tree htop
unzip sudo software-properties-common jq psmisc iproute python ssh rsync
gettext-base

# Install QNM
RUN mkdir -p workspace && cd workspace && wget
https://raw.githubusercontent.com/ConsenSys/QuorumNetworkManager/v0.7.5-bet
a/setup.sh && chmod +x setup.sh && ./setup.sh
ENV LANGUAGE=en_US.UTF-8 LC_ALL=en_US.UTF-8 LANG=en_US.UTF-8
RUN apt-get install -y locales && locale-gen en_US.UTF-8

WORKDIR /workspace/QuorumNetworkManager
ENTRYPOINT ["/bin/bash", "-i", "-c"]
```

The following is how the preceding Dockerfile works:

- We are using the Ubuntu `16.04` base image.
- We installed several basic utilities.
- We installed QNM using the command given at `https://github.com/ConsenSys/QuorumNetworkManager/releases/tag/v0.7.5-beta`.
- We set the working directory to `workspace/QuorumNetworkManager`, inside which we have the QNM files to start the node.
- We changed the entry point to use the `bash` shell instead of the `sh` shell because QNM doesn't work on the `sh` shell. QNM sets paths to various binaries in the `~/.bashrc` file, which is loaded by the bash shell when executed in interactive mode.

Go ahead and push the image to Docker Hub. I have pushed the image to `narayanprusty/qnm`.

Creating QNM deployment and service mainfest files

Let's write the mainfest file for creating deployments and services for QNM. We will create deployments for creating the Raft network only, but you can extend it to support IBFT without much hassle.

Here is the mainfest file to create a deployment and service for a Raft-based coordinating node:

```
apiVersion: apps/v1beta1
kind: Deployment
metadata:
  name: coordinator
spec:
  replicas: 1
  template:
    metadata:
      labels:
        app: coordinator
    spec:
      containers:
      - name: qnm
        image: narayanprusty/qnm
        args: ['node setupFromConfig.js']
        workingDir: /workspace/QuorumNetworkManager
        imagePullPolicy: Always
        env:
        - name: IP
          value: 0.0.0.0
        ports:
        - containerPort: 50000
        - containerPort: 50010
        - containerPort: 50020
        - containerPort: 20000
        - containerPort: 20010
        - containerPort: 20020
        - containerPort: 40000
        - containerPort: 30303
        - containerPort: 9000
---
kind: Service
apiVersion: v1
metadata:
  name: coordinator
spec:
```

```
ports:
    - name: remote-communication-node
      port: 50000
    - name: communication-node-rpc
      port: 50010
    - name: communication-node-ws-rpc
      port: 50020
    - name: geth-node
      port: 20000
    - name: geth-node-rpc
      port: 20010
    - name: geth-node-ws-rpc
      port: 20020
    - name: raft-http
      port: 40000
    - name: devp2p
      port: 30303
    - name: constellation
      port: 9000
selector:
    app: coordinator
type: NodePort
```

Here, the environmental various IP is used to indicate which IP the node should listen on. 0.0.0.0 indicates any IP. We are then exposing the ports that are opened by QNM. Everything in the preceding mainfest file is self-explanatory.

Now let's create the mainfest file for a dynamic peer:

```
apiVersion: apps/v1beta1
kind: Deployment
metadata:
  name: non-coordinator
spec:
  replicas: 1
  template:
    metadata:
      labels:
        app: non-coordinator
    spec:
      containers:
      - name: qnm
        image: narayanprusty/qnm
        args: ['node setupFromConfig.js']
        workingDir: /workspace/QuorumNetworkManager
        imagePullPolicy: Always
        env:
        - name: COORDINATING_IP
```

```
                    value: 10.97.145.237
                - name: ROLE
                    value: dynamicPeer
                - name: IP
                    value: 0.0.0.0
                ports:
                - containerPort: 50000
                - containerPort: 50010
                - containerPort: 50020
                - containerPort: 20000
                - containerPort: 20010
                - containerPort: 20020
                - containerPort: 40000
                - containerPort: 30303
                - containerPort: 9000
---
kind: Service
apiVersion: v1
metadata:
  name: non-coordinator
spec:
  ports:
    - name: remote-communication-node
      port: 50000
    - name: communication-node-rpc
      port: 50010
    - name: communication-node-ws-rpc
      port: 50020
    - name: geth-node
      port: 20000
    - name: geth-node-rpc
      port: 20010
    - name: geth-node-ws-rpc
      port: 20020
    - name: raft-http
      port: 40000
    - name: devp2p
      port: 30303
    - name: constellation
      port: 9000
  selector:
      app: non-coordinator
  type: NodePort
```

This mainfest file looks pretty similar to the previous mainfest file, except for the environmental variables. Here, we are providing the IP address of the coordinating node. The IP address is a cluster IP exposed by the coordinating peer service. It should be different for you. Then we have the ROLE environmental variable to indicate that QNM is a dynamic peer and not a coordinating peer.

Creating nodes using the K8s APIs

The K8s master exposes APIs that you can use to read and write K8s resource objects. You can find the API reference at `https://kubernetes.io/docs/reference/`. For QaaS, you would need to create a frontend that internally calls these APIs to create deployments and services.

The easiest way access the K8s APIs is through the HTTP proxy. Kubectl lets you create a proxy server between localhost and the K8s API Server. All incoming data enters through one port and gets forwarded to the remote K8s API Server port, except for the path matching the static content path. To create the proxy server, use the following command:

```
kubectl proxy --address="0.0.0.0" -p 8000
```

Let's see an example of how to create a deployment for the coordinator node using Node.js:

```
var request = require("request");

var options = {
    method: 'POST',
    url: 'http://127.0.0.1:8000/apis/apps/v1beta1/namespaces/
      default/deployments',
    headers: {
        'Content-Type': 'application/json'
    },
    body: {
        apiVersion: 'apps/v1beta1',
        kind: 'Deployment',
        metadata: {
            name: 'coordinator'
        },
        spec: {
            replicas: 1,
            template: {
                metadata: {
                    labels: {
                        app: 'coordinator'
```

```
                                    }
                                },
                                spec: {
                                    containers: [{
                                        name: 'qnm',
                                        image: 'narayanprusty/qnm',
                                        args: ['node setupFromConfig.js'],
                                        workingDir: '/workspace/QuorumNetworkManager',
                                        imagePullPolicy: 'Always',
                                        env: [{
                                            name: 'IP',
                                            value: '0.0.0.0'
                                        }],
                                        ports: [{
                                                containerPort: 50000
                                            },
                                            {
                                                containerPort: 50010
                                            },
                                            {
                                                containerPort: 50020
                                            },
                                            {
                                                containerPort: 20000
                                            },
                                            {
                                                containerPort: 20010
                                            },
                                            {
                                                containerPort: 20020
                                            },
                                            {
                                                containerPort: 40000
                                            },
                                            {
                                                containerPort: 30303
                                            },
                                            {
                                                containerPort: 9000
                                            }
                                        ]
                                    }]
                                }
                            }
                        }
                    },
                    json: true
                };
```

```
request(options, function(error, response, body) {
    if (error) throw new Error(error);

    console.log(body);
});
```

Similarly, let's see an example of how to create the service for the coordinating node using
Node.js:

```
var request = require("request");

var options = {
    method: 'POST',
    url: 'http://127.0.0.1:8000/api/v1/namespaces/default/services',
    headers: {
        'Content-Type': 'application/json'
    },
    body: {
        kind: 'Service',
        apiVersion: 'v1',
        metadata: {
            name: 'coordinator'
        },
        spec: {
            ports: [{
                    name: 'remote-communication-node',
                    port: 50000
                },
                {
                    name: 'communication-node-rpc',
                    port: 50010
                },
                {
                    name: 'communication-node-ws-rpc',
                    port: 50020
                },
                {
                    name: 'geth-node',
                    port: 20000
                },
                {
                    name: 'geth-node-rpc',
                    port: 20010
                },
                {
                    name: 'geth-node-ws-rpc',
                    port: 20020
                },
```

```
                {
                    name: 'raft-http',
                    port: 40000
                },
                {
                    name: 'devp2p',
                    port: 30303
                },
                {
                    name: 'constellation',
                    port: 9000
                }
            ],
            selector: {
                app: 'coordinator'
            },
            type: 'NodePort'
        }
    },
    json: true
};

request(options, function(error, response, body) {
    if (error) throw new Error(error);

    console.log(body);
});
```

Summary

In this chapter, we learned the basics of cloud computing and containerization through examples. We looked at the importance of containerization and how to containerize an application using Docker. We then saw the importance of K8s and how it makes it easy to build microservices-architecture-based applications. After that, we learned how to install minikube and deploy containers on K8s.

Finally, we used all the skills we learned to develop a QaaS as a Service using QNM. In the next chapter, we will create a basic UI for the QaaS that calls the K8s APIs to create and join networks.

7
Building a DApp for Digitizing Medical Records

The whole health industry is filled with a great many paper-based medical records, which is causing huge losses in terms of money, time, and lives. **Electronic Medical Records (EMRs)** are the solutions to many of the problems caused by paper records. There are many companies and researchers working on building EMR data management and sharing systems using blockchain technology. We will design a very different solution than the ones you will find on the internet, in the sense that those are focused only on anonymity, access control, security, and privacy, whereas our solution will also provide user experience and mass adoptability by enabling cross-application communication. While building the system, we will learn how to achieve privacy using **Proxy Re-Encryption** (PRE).

In this chapter, we will learn about the following topics:

- What a healthcare data management system is and what its functionalities are?
- The problems caused by paper medical records and the benefits of digitalized medical records
- The limitations of healthcare data management systems?
- The problems with building a centralized healthcare data management application
- What PRE is and how it helps to achieve data privacy in a blockchain
- How to architect a decentralized healthcare data management system that enables cross-application data sharing
- How to build smart contracts and tests for a healthcare data management, DApp, using Python and JavaScript

Introduction to EMRs data management and sharing systems

EMRs consist of critical, highly sensitive private information in healthcare, and need to be frequently shared among peers. EMR data management and sharing systems facilitate secure and trustable ways for different actors to read and write EMRs to the system. These systems should ensure privacy, security, availability, and fine-grained access control over EMR data. EMRs include prescriptions, lab reports, bills, and any other paper-based record that you can find in hospitals.

In general, an EMR data management and sharing system allow doctors to issue digital prescriptions, pharmacies to pull prescriptions based on a patient's identity, labs to issue digital reports, patients to see all their records and share them with others, and so on.

Problems with paper-based medical records

Medical records need to be distributed and shared among peers, such as healthcare providers, insurance companies, pharmacies, researchers, and patients' families, which is a challenge in itself. Even after sharing, these records need to be constantly updated during the treatment process. It's also easier to lose or misplace paper records. When someone is suffering from a serious medical condition, such as cancer or HIV, they have to maintain a long history of records as this is crucial for the treatment. With paper records, it's cumbersome to maintain a long history of records.

In addition, forged health records are submitted to insurance companies, resulting in huge financial losses to the insurance companies. Many times, doctors and labs also issue fake prescriptions and records to patients with patients' consent. For example, universities require students to pass several tests before being admitted, and sometimes students try to get fake reports without going through the tests.

Many patients don't buy their medication, and there is no way to track whether a patient has consumed the necessary medicines. This results in harm being done to the patient's quality of life and an increased cost to the healthcare system. If a patient is visiting different doctors, then there is a huge chance of harmful side effects due to different types of medicines recommended by different doctors. If an individual has multiple doctors treating them, then there is no way for these doctors to work together on the patient's medicine management plan, therefore making it impossible to streamline the entire process for all involved parties. Because of a patient's failure to present their past records, tests related to allergies due to particular chemicals or substances need to be done again and again when visiting different clinics, which is not needed if the patient's medical history is maintained.

Bad handwriting in prescriptionscan also create a risk of medication errors. Also, due to oral communication between doctors when there is remote communication, there is a huge chance of medication errors. Also, due to a prescriber's insufficient knowledge of the desired dosage of a drug, or undesired interactions between multiple drugs. There is also no way to implement warning and alert systems in paper prescriptions.

It's difficult for research companies to collect and structure medical records for research purposes. There is no way to renew a prescription after finishing medicines, so the patient will need a doctor again, which is a cumbersome process. Paper subscriptions have failed to enable purchase medicines online, but digital subscriptions can open the door for online medicine delivery as prescriptions can be verified online.

An EMR data management and sharing system should aim to solve a few or all of the previous problems. For example, in the case of prescription renewal, the first step is to digitize the prescription. Then, on the patient's request, pharmacy staff can generate a renewal request that is delivered to the prescriber. The prescriber can then review the request and act accordingly by approving or denying the request. With limited resource utilization and just a few clicks from the prescriber, they can complete a medication renewal task while enhancing continuous patient documentation.

The previous issues are just a few of the problems caused by paper-based records. But the whole healthcare industry is filled with a huge number of problems due to paper-based records. A solution should be designed in such a way that it solves these problems, and could be enhanced regularly to solve additional problems.

Limitations of EMR data management and sharing systems

Though an EMR data management and sharing system solves a lot of problems, it has some limitations that effect its adaptability and the trust that people place in it. The following are some of the limitations:

- **Financial cost and return on investment**: The costs of purchasing, implementing, supporting, and maintaining such a system are unaffordable, especially for small hospitals and clinics. Even if they are given the system for free, there are other financial costs related to the management of the interface, customization for flexibility, training, maintenance, and upgrades.

- **Upgrading the workforce**: Currently, the workforce is addicted to paper-based records. Training patients, doctors, pharmacies, hospitals, and so on to adopt the solution is a difficult and time-consuming task. Sometimes it may require changing the workforce. For example, when banks started implementing computers, transitioning from record-keeping books to digital records, a lot of people couldn't understand and adopt it and therefore lost jobs.
- **Integrity of data input**: Accidental data entry errors, such as selecting the wrong patient or clicking on the wrong choice in a menu of dosages, may occur.
- **Security and privacy**: This is one of the most important concerns. Health records need to be stored securely as eHealth databases are always a target of hackers. Health records contain very sensitive information, and leakage could result in catastrophe. Strong access control should be implemented and regular feedback should be taken. Without the patient's consent, their records should not be shared with anyone.
- **System downtime**: There are chances of regular system downtime due to network or hardware related issues. The inability to use the system is of great concern.
- **Lost patient access**: In the event of a development beyond the control of the patient, such as a software malfunction in the healthcare provider's office, the patient can no longer ask the care provider for a paper script to take to a pharmacy in order to obtain needed medicines. This leaves the patient at the mercy of technicians or other undiscoverable workers.

Centralized versus decentralized EMR management systems

Regardless of whether an EMR management system is centralized or decentralized, it has to be compliant with a health authority's laws. Because of the fact that it's sensitive public data, there should be a regulatory body to define the standards and dictate the rules of how the data is shared and stored. For example, the **Health Insurance Portability and Accountability Act (HIPAA)** of 1996 is United States legislation that provides data privacy and security provisions for safeguarding medical information. Similarly, different countries have different legislation.

To understand what the problem is with centralized EMR data management apps, let's take an example of the Google Health centralized service. The Google Health service allowed users to add their health records to the app either manually or by logging in to Google's partnered health service providers. Records stored in the app could include health conditions, medications, allergies, and lab results. Google Health used the information to provide the users with information on medical conditions and possible interactions between drugs, conditions, and allergies.

In 2011, Google announced it was retiring Google Health in January 1, 2012. Data was available for download through to January 1, 2013. The reason Google gave for abandoning the project was the lack of widespread adoption.

This shows that it's difficult for us to trust centralized apps as they can discontinue the service at any time. As a patient, this is a big concern as suddenly you have to look for a different option to manage your records. Even hospitals and other health service providers will have to change their system. Even if you wish to switch to a different app, migrating the data is not easy. Many Google Health customers moved to using Microsoft HealthVault, which was a competing service. Microsoft released a tool that let Google Health customers transfer their personal health information to a Microsoft HealthVault account. But what if Microsoft also stops their service? Therefore, centralized health applications built by private companies cannot be trusted and adopted.

Because of this, many governments have come up with their own centralized services. An example of this is the e-prescriptions service of Estonia. Government services can be trusted, and adoption is not a problem because of the fact that governments can make it compulsory for health service providers to use the service. They are the authority to mandate this. But the problem is that one app cannot solve all problems, provide the best set of features, have the best user experience, and so on.

Both government and private centralized apps have issues for example, in the event of a security breach, hackers could compromise all public records in centralized services. Also, what's the guarantee that the health records will not be modified or that certain records are not removed by the central server?

The preceding concerns mean that we need to design a decentralized system using a blockchain, where blockchain is used for EMR access control and identity management only, and where the EMRs reside in a centralized and distributed storage. All of the apps connected to this network can talk to each other and share data. Users can switch between the apps easily and the health authority will be able to regulate and monitor the network. For example, two different service provides can build different apps with different sets of features and user experiences, but users of the different apps can read/write to each app's EMRs.

The health authority decides who joins the network and can provide healthcare apps. To join the network, the health authority can set a precheck list of standards and measures that the apps should meet in order to be able to join the network.

Ensuring data privacy in a blockchain using PRE

Before getting any further and building our decentralized EMR data management and sharing system, let's learn about what PRE is. In our solution, we will be using PRE to ensure security and privacy.

PRE is a set of algorithms that allows you to encrypt some text with your key and then alter the ciphertext so that it can be decrypted by another party without revealing your key. To alter the ciphertext, you need the other party's private or public key, based on whether you are using interactive or noninteractive PRE algorithms, respectively. Regardless of the algorithm, PRE involves generating a re-encrypt key, which is used to re-encrypt the data. The re-encrypt key is generated based on the owner's private key and the recipient's private or public key, based on the type of algorithm.

In practice, PRE is used to store sensitive data on a third-party server and lets you decide who gets access to the data without revealing the actual data to the third-party server. PRE allows third parties (proxies) to alter a ciphertext that has been encrypted for one party so that it can be decrypted by another party.

Rather than naively sharing your private key with recipients (insecure) or encrypting the entire message n times for each recipient, PRE allows you to encrypt the data once and then delegate access to it based on the recipients' public keys. This removes the requirement for the data owner to be online (data can stored in a different server, which you don't have to manage) and also facilitates the revocation of access (to block access, you can run PRE again to change your keys and then delete the old ciphertext).

The PRE algorithm that NuCypher PRE currently supports is BBS98. BBS98 is based on elliptic curve cryptography. This library, by default, uses the secp256k1 curve. Note that the Ethereum accounts also use the same curve (secp256k1), so we can use the Ethereum account keys with NuCypher.

Currently, the field of PRE is still under heavily researched and developed. There aren't many libraries available for PRE. You will find Java or Python-based libraries for interactive PRE, but for non-interactive—or symmetric key-based, you won't find any. Because of this limitation, we will adhere to a microservices architecture and move all proxy re-encrypted code to a Python-based microservice.

The NuCypher PRE library

NuCypher is a company that has built a decentralized PRE as a service product called NuCypher **Key Management Service (KMS)**. NuCypher KMS is a decentralized KMS, encryption, and access control service. It enables private data sharing between arbitrary numbers of participants in public networks, using PRE to delegate decryption rights in a way that cannot be achieved by traditional symmetric or public key encryption schemes. Native tokens are used to **incentivize network** participants to perform key management and access delegation/revocation operations.

We won't be going through NuCypher KMS in depth or using it in this book. Instead, we will explore how to use the PRE library built by NuCypher. NuCypher provides PRE libraries for Python and Java, but we will only learn how to use the Python PRE library.

 NuCypher is not the only Python library available for PRE. There are a few others out there. For example, ZeroDB also provides a PRE library that supports the AFGH algorithm, which is a non-interactive PRE algorithm. You can find out more about it at: `https://github.com/zerodb/zerodb-afgh-pre`.

Installing the library

This library requires `python3`, `libssl-dev`, and `libgmp-dev` as prerequisites. To install these on Ubuntu, run the following commands:

```
sudo apt-get install build-essential
sudo apt-get install python3
sudo apt-get install python3-dev libssl-dev libgmp-dev
```

Use the following commands on macOS:

```
brew install python3
brew install gmp
```

Now let's install the PRE library. To install it, run the following commands:

```
git clone https://github.com/nucypher/nucypher-pre-python.git
cd nucypher-pre-python
pip3 install -e .
```

Using the library

Let's see an example of how to use this library. This library supports only interactive algorithms; it requires the sender to know about the recipient's private key.

We will create a sample Python script where **Alice** will encrypt some text, **Bob** will share his private key with **Alice**, **Alice** will create a derivation key with **Bob** private key, then the **Proxy** will re-encrypt using the derivation key, and finally the re-encrypted data will be decrypted by **Bob** using his private key:

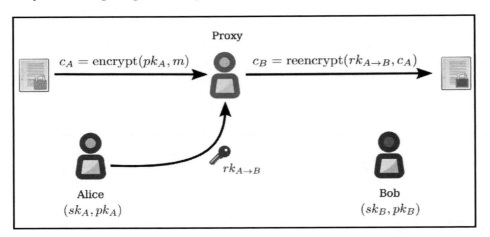

Here is the code for these interactions:

```
# Import bbs98 from NuCypher PRE
from npre import bbs98
# Initialize the re-encryption object
pre = bbs98.PRE()

# 'sk' means "secret key", and 'pk' means "public key"

# Alice's Private key
sk_a = pre.gen_priv(dtype=bytes)
# Alice's Public Key
pk_a = pre.priv2pub(sk_a)
```

```
# Bob's Private Key
sk_b = pre.gen_priv(dtype=bytes)
# Bob's Public Key
pk_b = pre.priv2pub(sk_b)

# Print Alice's Private Key as Hex String
print(sk_a.hex()[2:])
# Print Bob's Private Key as Hex String
print(sk_b.hex()[2:])

# Encrypt Message using Alice's Public Key
emsg = pre.encrypt(pk_a, "Hello World")

# Generate Re-Encrypt Key using Private key of sender and receiver
re_ab = pre.rekey(sk_a, sk_b)
# Re-Encrypt Message using Re-Encrypt key
emsg_b = pre.reencrypt(re_ab, emsg)

# Decrypt the message using Bob's Private Key
dmsg = pre.decrypt(sk_b, emsg_b)
# Print Decrypted Message
print(dmsg.decode("utf-8"))
```

The preceding code is self-explanatory. But the problem in the preceding scenario is that, for Alice to give access to the data to Bob, Alice needs to know Bob's private key. This is not an ideal situation and Bob may not be comfortable with sharing his key. For example, if Bob is using the same key for making blockchain transactions, then he would surely not want to share the key with Alice.

Luckily, there is a workaround: The trick involves Alice generating a new key pair, giving access to that key pair, and then sharing that key pair by encrypting it with Bob's public key. We will see this in practice later in this chapter.

Architecting DApp for EMRs

Let's design the architect of the DApp for enabling healthcare applications to share data with each other. Basically, users with different healthcare apps can share EMRs with each other.

The ecosystem of this app will consist of healthcare service providers (such as hospitals, labs, and insurance companies), patients, app providers (the companies that will build healthcare apps integrated with this blockchain network), and a network authority or administrator (the health authority and/or solution provider).

The following diagram shows the high-level architecture:

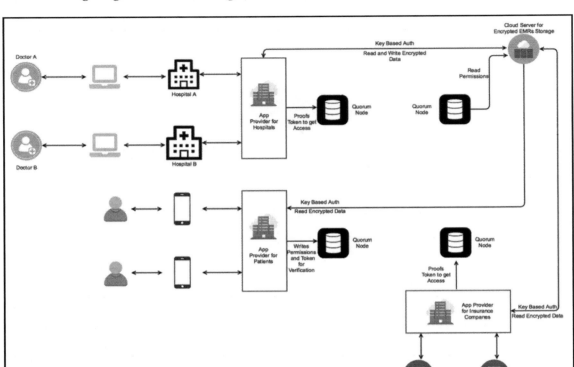

This is how the preceding architecture works:

- The administrator of the network decides who can join the network and connect to the Cloud server.

- The blockchain will hold the service providers and patients' identities and permissions, whereas the centralized and distributed server will store the encrypted EMRs. Every user and service provider will have their own Ethereum keys to identify themselves. There are two reasons why we are not storing the encrypted EMRs in the blockchain itself:
  - Every piece of data will be replicated to every node in the blockchain. This will harm scalability as the node size will increase drastically.

- According to compliance, you are not supposed to even share encrypted data, as encryption algorithms may break in the future and all of the data will get leaked. So, if it's kept in a central location, then the server can be unplugged immediately.

- Whenever someone requests data from the storage, the server will check the blockchain to see whether the patient has granted access, and if so, then it will re-encrypt it using the re-encryption key and give the re-encrypted data to the recipient.

- While asking to read or write data to the Cloud server, the client should sign a token provided by the server to prove their identity. Based on this, the Cloud server will look for permissions in the blockchain and decide whether to re-encrypt or not. The client will sign using their private Ethereum key. This is the process of authentication to the Cloud server.

- The user will register their identity on the blockchain. If a patient wants to give access to their data, then they will generate a new private key and a random token. Using this private key, the patient will generate a re-encrypt key and put it on the blockchain for the Cloud server to refer to while re-encrypting data. The user cannot generate the re-encrypt key directly using the service provider's key because, in that case, the service provider has to expose their private key, as we are using the interactive PRE algorithm. The random token's hash will be added to the blockchain by the patient and the service provider has to send a transaction proving that they know the random token acts as a proof that the user has shared access. This is a method of authorization to give data access. For example, if a user wants to give access to their EMRs on a mobile phone, then the user will generate a QR code, which has a private key and token. Then they will send the transaction to the blockchain, stating that whoever proves they have the token will be given access to their data. At the hospital, the receptionist can simply scan the QR code and push a transaction proofing to acquire the random string, thereby gaining access to the user's data. The QR code will also hold the private key. Every time the patient wants to give someone access, they have to generate a new key pair and token.

- Once write access is granted, the service provider can create EMRs of a defined format, put their hash on the blockchain, and send the EMR—which is encrypted using the patient's public key to the Cloud server for storage.

- The Cloud server is controlled by the health authority or by the solution provider. It should be health-authority-compliant and should adhere to the standards. Even if the Cloud server gets hacked, the hackers won't be able to read anything because everything that is stored in it is encrypted and the keys are distributed across various app providers.
- The solution can be extended in such a way that the end users control their private keys so that they don't have to trust the app provider. But this will harm the user experience, as users are not used to storing private keys. If they lose the key, then access to their EMRs is lost forever.
- Although the Cloud server creates centralization for accessing the EMRs, you can still trust it. The keys aren't stored in the Cloud server—it just acts as storage. Even if the Cloud server gives access to your data to someone without your permission, the recipient cannot read the data, so the Cloud server can be trusted. This server can be distributed to achieve high availability.
- This solution allows you to use different healthcare apps from different app providers and still have visibility of all the EMRs on each of the apps. To import all EMRs on a new app, a user has to export the key from the previous app and import it on the new app.

One issue that still exists is: how would you revoke access after granting access to someone? Of course, you can revoke the access on the blockchain, but what if the Cloud server still gives access to your new EMRs to the service provider? There is very little chance this would happen as it is unlikely any incentive for the Cloud server to do this. But this can be avoided by patients if they change their keys and run PRE on their data. This will invalidate all the re-encrypt keys you have shared so far, therefore new EMRs cannot be read by the existing service providers that you had given access to in the past.

Smart contracts for identity and access control

Let's write the smart contracts that will be responsible for registering the identity of patients and service providers, and for providing access control.

Here is the smart contract code:

```
pragma solidity ^0.4.22;

contract Health {

    address owner;
```

```
struct ServiceProvider {
    string publicKey;
}

struct Permission {
    bool read;
    bool write;
    string reEncKey; //Re-Encrypt Key
}

struct Token {
    int status;
    bool read;
    bool write;
    string reEncKey; //Re-Encrypt Key
}

struct EMR {
    string hash;
    address issuer;
}

struct Patient {
    string publicKey;
    mapping (address => Permission) permissions;
    mapping (bytes32 => Token) tokens;
    bool closed;
    EMR[] EMRs;
}

mapping (address => ServiceProvider) serviceProviders;
mapping (address => Patient) patients;

event tokenVerified (bytes32 hash, address patient, address
   serviceProvider);
event reEncKeyAdded (address patient, address serviceProvider);
event patientAccountChanged(address oldAccountAddress, string
   oldAccountPublicKey, address newAccountAddress, string
   newAccountPublicKey, string reEncKey);
event emrAdded(address patient, address serviceProvider,
   string emrHash);

constructor() {
    owner = msg.sender;
}

//Utilities
function fromHexChar(uint c) public pure returns (uint) {
```

```
        if (byte(c) >= byte('0') && byte(c) <= byte('9')) {
            return c - uint(byte('0'));
        }
        if (byte(c) >= byte('a') && byte(c) <= byte('f')) {
            return 10 + c - uint(byte('a'));
        }
        if (byte(c) >= byte('A') && byte(c) <= byte('F')) {
            return 10 + c - uint(byte('A'));
        }
    }

    function fromHex(string s) public pure returns (bytes) {
        bytes memory ss = bytes(s);
        require(ss.length%2 == 0); // length must be even
        bytes memory r = new bytes(ss.length/2);
        for (uint i=0; i<ss.length/2; ++i) {
            r[i] = byte(fromHexChar(uint(ss[2*i])) * 16 +
                        fromHexChar(uint(ss[2*i+1])));
        }
        return r;
    }

    //Register Patient
    function addPatient(string publicKey) returns (int reason) {
        if(address(keccak256(fromHex(publicKey))) == msg.sender) {
            patients[msg.sender].publicKey = publicKey;
        }
    }

    //Register Service provider
    function addServiceProvider(string publicKey) {
        if(address(keccak256(fromHex(publicKey))) == msg.sender) {
            serviceProviders[msg.sender].publicKey = publicKey;
        }
    }

    //Patient:
    //In QRCode include token string, address and private key
    //Adds the hash of token and derivation key in Blockchain
    function addToken(bytes32 hash, bool read, bool write, string reEncKey)
    {
        if(patients[msg.sender].tokens[hash].status == 0 &&
          patients[msg.sender].closed == false) {
            patients[msg.sender].tokens[hash].status = 1;
            patients[msg.sender].tokens[hash].read = read;
            patients[msg.sender].tokens[hash].write = write;
            patients[msg.sender].tokens[hash].reEncKey = reEncKey;
        }
```

```
    }

    //Service Provider proves the token to get access
    function requestAccess(string token, address patient) {
        bytes32 hash = sha256(token);
        if(patients[patient].tokens[hash].status == 1) {
            patients[patient].tokens[hash].status = 2;
            patients[patient].permissions[msg.sender].read =
                patients[patient].tokens[hash].read;
            patients[patient].permissions[msg.sender].write =
                patients[patient].tokens[hash].write;
            patients[patient].permissions[msg.sender].reEncKey =
                patients[patient].tokens[hash].reEncKey;
            tokenVerified(hash, patient, msg.sender);
        }
    }

    //Add EMR
    function addEMR(address patient, string hash) {
        if(patients[patient].permissions[msg.sender].write == true) {
            patients[patient].EMRs.push(EMR(hash, msg.sender));
            emrAdded(patient, msg.sender, hash);
        }
    }

    function getPatientPublicKey(address patient) returns
      (string publicKey) {
        return patients[patient].publicKey;
    }

    function isPatientProfileClosed(address patient) returns
      (bool isClosed) {
        return patients[patient].closed;
    }

    function getServiceProviderPublicKey(address serviceProvider)
      returns (string publicKey) {
        return serviceProviders[serviceProvider].publicKey;
    }

    //Revoke Access. Here you aren't changing the key.
    function revokeServiceProviderAccess(address serviceProvider) {
        patients[msg.sender].permissions[serviceProvider].read = false;
        patients[msg.sender].permissions[serviceProvider].write =
        false;
    }

    function getPermission(address patient, address serviceProvider)
```

```
        returns(bool read, bool write, string reEncKey) {
          return (patients[patient].permissions[serviceProvider].read,
            patients[patient].permissions[serviceProvider].read,
            patients[patient].permissions[serviceProvider].reEncKey);
    }

    function getToken(address patient, bytes32 hash) returns (int
      status, bool read, bool write, string reEncKey) {
          return (patients[patient].tokens[hash].status,
            patients[patient].tokens[hash].read,
            patients[patient].tokens[hash].write,
            patients[patient].tokens[hash].reEncKey);
    }

    //Change your keys to revoke old account and move EMRs to new
    // account.
    function changePatientAccount(string reEncKey,
      address newAddress, string newPublicKey) {
          patients[msg.sender].closed = true;
          if(address(keccak256(fromHex(newPublicKey))) == newAddress) {
              patients[newAddress].publicKey = newPublicKey;
              patientAccountChanged(msg.sender,
                patients[msg.sender].publicKey, newAddress,
                newPublicKey, reEncKey);
          }
      }
  }
}
```

Most of the code in the preceding smart contract is self-explanatory. While registering patients and service providers, we are passing the public key and also verifying whether the public key is correct. `address(keccak256(fromHex(publicKey))` phrase calculates `address` from `publicKey`. `changePatientAccount` is used to change the account keys of the user, in case the keys are compromised. For example, this can be used if your app provider's servers get hacked and your private keys get leaked; the app provider can use this functionality to deactivate previous accounts and generate new ones for the users. The Cloud server will look for the `patientAccountChanged` event and run re-encryption on your encrypted EMRs so that you can access them with the new key. It will then delete the old encrypted EMRs. This can also be used by users to revoke access to the EMRs from all service providers.

Writing Python and JS scripts for testing

Let's now write some test scripts to test the smart contract and the data and user flow. We will write Python scripts to encrypt data, decrypt data, generate a re-encryption key, and re-encrypt data. And we will use Node.js to invoke the Python scripts and smart contract functions.

Create a directory named `test`. In this, create a file named `encrypt.py` and place the following code into it:

```
from npre import bbs98
pre = bbs98.PRE()
import base64
import sys

publicKey = base64.b64decode(sys.argv[1])
encrypted_message = pre.encrypt(publicKey, sys.argv[2])

print(base64.b64encode(encrypted_message))
```

This script takes two arguments, `publicKey` and a raw message. `publicKey` is passed as a `base64` encoded public key. This script converts the public key to bytes so that the `npre` library can utilize it. Finally, it encrypts the message and prints it as a `base64` encoded ciphertext.

Create another file called `decrypt.py` and place the following code into it:

```
from npre import bbs98
pre = bbs98.PRE()
import base64
import sys

privateKey = base64.b64decode(sys.argv[1])
encrypted_message = base64.b64decode(sys.argv[2])

decrypted_message = pre.decrypt(privateKey, encrypted_message)

print(decrypted_message)
```

This code is responsible for decryption. Now, create another file called `generate_reEncKey.py` and place the following code in it:

```
from npre import bbs98
pre = bbs98.PRE()
import base64
import sys
```

```
base64_privateKeyA = base64.b64decode(sys.argv[1])
base64_privateKeyB = base64.b64decode(sys.argv[2])

re_ab = pre.rekey(base64_privateKeyA, base64_privateKeyB)

print(base64.b64encode(re_ab))
```

This code is responsible for generating the re-encryption key. Now, create another file called re_encrypt.py and place the following code into it:

```
from npre import bbs98
pre = bbs98.PRE()
import base64
import sys

reEncryptKey = base64.b64decode(sys.argv[1])
encrypted_message = base64.b64decode(sys.argv[2])
re_encrypted_message = pre.reencrypt(reEncryptKey, encrypted_message)

print(base64.b64encode(re_encrypted_message))
```

This code is responsible for re-encrypting the ciphertext. Now create a package.json file, which will hold the dependencies of our Node.js app. Place the following content in the file and run the npm install command to install the modules:

```
{
    "name": "health",
    "private": true,
    "dependencies": {
        "eth-crypto": "^1.2.1",
        "ethereumjs-tx": "~1.3.4",
        "ethereumjs-util": "~5.2.0",
        "ethereumjs-wallet": "~0.6.0",
        "sha256": "~0.2.0",
        "web3": "^0.20.6",
        "child_process": "~1.0.2"
    }
}
```

Now, finally, create a file named app.js and place within it the following test code:

```
let Web3 = require("web3");
let ethereumjsWallet = require("ethereumjs-wallet")
let ethereumjsUtil = require("ethereumjs-util");
let ethereumjsTx = require("ethereumjs-tx");
let sha256 = require("sha256");
let EthCrypto = require('eth-crypto');
let exec = require("child_process").exec;
```

```
let web3 = new Web3(new
  Web3.providers.HttpProvider("http://localhost:8545"));

let healthContract = web3.eth.contract([]);
let health = healthContract.new({
  from: web3.eth.accounts[0],
  data: '0x608060aa31862e....',
  gas: '4700000'
}, function(e, contract) {
  if (typeof contract.address !== 'undefined') {
    let healthContractInstance = healthContract.at(contract.address);

    //Generate Patient's Keys
    let patient_wallet = ethereumjsWallet.generate();

    //Register the Patient on blockchain.
    let data = healthContractInstance.addPatient.getData
      (patient_wallet.getPublicKey().toString('hex'));
    let nonce = web3.eth.getTransactionCount
      (patient_wallet.getAddressString())

    let rawTx = {
      gasPrice: web3.toHex(web3.eth.gasPrice),
      gasLimit: web3.toHex(4700000),
      from: patient_wallet.getAddressString(),
      nonce: web3.toHex(nonce),
      data: data,
      to: contract.address
    };

    let privateKey = ethereumjsUtil.toBuffer("0x" +
      patient_wallet.getPrivateKey().toString('hex'), 'hex');
    let tx = new ethereumjsTx(rawTx);
    tx.sign(privateKey);

    web3.eth.sendRawTransaction("0x" + tx.serialize().toString('hex'),
      function(error, result) {
      if (error) {
        console.log(error)
        res.status(500).send({
          error: "An error occured"
        })
      } else {
        console.log("Patient Pub Key: " +
          healthContractInstance.getPatientPublicKey.call
          (patient_wallet.getAddressString()))

        //Generate Service Provider's Keys
```

```
        let hospital_wallet = ethereumjsWallet.generate();

        //continue from here
      }
    })
  }
})
```

Compile the smart contract and populate the `healthContract` and `health` variables with the ABI and bytecode respectively.

Here is how the preceding code works:

- We use the `ethereumjs` libraries for creating offline accounts and signing transactions using those accounts.
- We use `child_process` to execute Python scripts from Node.js. Though you can use RESTful APIs and adopt a microservices architecture, for testing purposes, this is fine.
- We use `EthCrypto` to compress and uncompress the public key. The public key generated by `ethereumjs-wallet` is uncompressed, whereas the public key that is generated and used by `npre` is compressed. Private keys are always 32 bytes, and public keys are always 65 bytes (or 33 bytes for a compressed public key). Public key hashes are always 20 bytes. `npre` also adds `0x00` in the beginning of a private key and `0x01` in the beginning of a public key.
- At first, we generate a patient's wallet and register it on the blockchain. In a real application, you can also register the user profile and service provider on the Cloud server. The user profile can contain details such as the name, age, and other details on patients; similarly, the service provider profile can contain license numbers, names, and so on. These profiles can be encrypted using the owner's public key and stored on the Cloud server.

Now, insert the following code where we have a continuation comment:

```
//Generate Service Provider's Keys
let hospital_wallet = ethereumjsWallet.generate();

//Register the Service Provider on blockchain
let data = healthContractInstance.addServiceProvider.getData
  (hospital_wallet.getPublicKey().toString('hex'));
let nonce = web3.eth.getTransactionCount
  (hospital_wallet.getAddressString())

let rawTx = {
  gasPrice: web3.toHex(web3.eth.gasPrice),
```

```
    gasLimit: web3.toHex(4700000),
    from: hospital_wallet.getAddressString(),
    nonce: web3.toHex(nonce),
    data: data,
    to: contract.address
};

let privateKey = ethereumjsUtil.toBuffer("0x" +
    hospital_wallet.getPrivateKey().toString('hex'), 'hex');
let tx = new ethereumjsTx(rawTx);
tx.sign(privateKey);

web3.eth.sendRawTransaction("0x" + tx.serialize().toString('hex'),
    function(error, result) {
    if (error) {
      console.log(error)
    } else {
      console.log("Hospital Pub Key: " +
        healthContractInstance.getServiceProviderPublicKey.call
        (hospital_wallet.getAddressString()))

      let token = "yr238932";
      let tokenHash = "0x" + sha256(token);

      //Generate private key like npre. It has a extra character 0x00
      //in beginning
      let secKeyA = Buffer.concat([new Buffer([0x00]),
        patient_wallet.getPrivateKey()]).toString('base64')
      //Generate another private key to share with service provider
      let temp_wallet = ethereumjsWallet.generate();
      let secKeyB = Buffer.concat([new Buffer([0x00]),
        temp_wallet.getPrivateKey()]).toString('base64')

      exec('python3 ./generate_reEncKey.py ' + secKeyA + " " + secKeyB,
        (error, stdout, stderr) => {
        if (error !== null) {
          console.log(error)
        } else {
          let reEncKey = stdout.substr(2).slice(0, -2)

          console.log("Re-Encryption Key: " + reEncKey)

          //Add token to blockchain
          let data = healthContractInstance.addToken.getData
            (tokenHash, true, true, reEncKey);
          let nonce = web3.eth.getTransactionCount
            (patient_wallet.getAddressString())
```

```
let rawTx = {
  gasPrice: web3.toHex(web3.eth.gasPrice),
  gasLimit: web3.toHex(4700000),
  from: patient_wallet.getAddressString(),
  nonce: web3.toHex(nonce),
  data: data,
  to: contract.address
};

let privateKey = ethereumjsUtil.toBuffer("0x" +
  patient_wallet.getPrivateKey().toString('hex'), 'hex');
let tx = new ethereumjsTx(rawTx);
tx.sign(privateKey);

web3.eth.sendRawTransaction("0x" +
  tx.serialize().toString('hex'),
  function(error, result) {
  if (error) {
    console.log(error)
  } else {
    console.log("Token Info: " +
      healthContractInstance.getToken.call
      (patient_wallet.getAddressString(), tokenHash, {
      from: patient_wallet.getAddressString()
    }))

    //Get access to patient's data
    let data =
      healthContractInstance.requestAccess.getData
      (token, patient_wallet.getAddressString());
    let nonce = web3.eth.getTransactionCount
      (hospital_wallet.getAddressString())

    let rawTx = {
      gasPrice: web3.toHex(web3.eth.gasPrice),
      gasLimit: web3.toHex(4700000),
      from: hospital_wallet.getAddressString(),
      nonce: web3.toHex(nonce),
      data: data,
      to: contract.address
    };

    let privateKey = ethereumjsUtil.toBuffer("0x" +
      hospital_wallet.getPrivateKey().toString('hex'),
      'hex');
    let tx = new ethereumjsTx(rawTx);
    tx.sign(privateKey);
```

```
web3.eth.sendRawTransaction("0x" +
  tx.serialize().toString('hex'),
  function(error, result) {
  if (error) {
    console.log(error)
  } else {
    console.log("Permission Info: " +
      healthContractInstance.getPermission.call
      (patient_wallet.getAddressString(),
      hospital_wallet.getAddressString(), {
      from: hospital_wallet.getAddressString()
    }))

  }
})
}
})
}
})
}
})
```

Here, we generated a temporary key pair and assumed that it's shared with the service provider. Then, we generated a re-encrypt key using the patient's private key and a temporary private key. Then, we made a `addToken` transaction from the patient's wallet and a `requestAccess` transaction from the service provider's wallet. These two transactions provide the service provider with access to the patient's EMRs.

Now insert the following code where we have a continuation comment:

```
let emr = JSON.stringify({
  "Blood Group": "O+",
  "type": "Blood Report"
});
let emrHash = sha256(emr);

let data = healthContractInstance.addEMR.getData
  (patient_wallet.getAddressString(), emrHash);
let nonce = web3.eth.getTransactionCount
  (hospital_wallet.getAddressString())

let rawTx = {
  gasPrice: web3.toHex(web3.eth.gasPrice),
  gasLimit: web3.toHex(4700000),
  from: hospital_wallet.getAddressString(),
  nonce: web3.toHex(nonce),
  data: data,
```

```
    to: contract.address
};

let privateKey = ethereumjsUtil.toBuffer("0x" +
hospital_wallet.getPrivateKey().toString('hex'), 'hex');
let tx = new ethereumjsTx(rawTx);
tx.sign(privateKey);

web3.eth.sendRawTransaction("0x" + tx.serialize().toString('hex'),
  function(error, result) {
    if (error) {
      console.log(error)
    } else {
      //Generate Public Key like npre. It's compressed and has a
      //extra character 0x01 in beginning
      let compressedPublicKey = Buffer.concat
        ([new Buffer([0x01]), Buffer.from(EthCrypto.publicKey.compress
        (patient_wallet.getPublicKey().toString("hex")),
        'hex')]).toString("base64")

      exec('python3 ./encrypt.py ' + compressedPublicKey + " '" +
        emr + "'", (error, stdout, stderr) => {
        if (error !== null) {
          console.log(error)
        } else {
          //Assume we are pushing encrypted data to proxy
          //re-encryption server
          let encryptedEMR = stdout.substr(2).slice(0, -2);
          console.log("Encrypted Message: " + encryptedEMR)

          //Assume that proxy re-encryption server re-encrypting
          // data when requested by authorized service provider
          exec('python3 ./re_encrypt.py ' + reEncKey + " " +
            encryptedEMR, (error, stdout, stderr) => {
            if (error !== null) {
              console.log(error)
            } else {
              let reEncryptedEMR = stdout.substr(2).slice(0, -2)
              console.log("Re-Encrypted Message: " + reEncryptedEMR)

              //Assume service provider decrypting the re-encrypted
              //data provided by the proxy re-encryption server
              exec('python3 ./decrypt.py ' + secKeyB + " " +
                reEncryptedEMR, (error, stdout, stderr) => {
                if (error) {
                  console.log(error)
                } else {
                  let decrypted_message = stdout.substr(2).slice(0, -2)
```

```
console.log("Decrypted Message: " + decrypted_message)

//Generate a new key for patient
let new_patient_wallet = ethereumjsWallet.generate();

let secKeyA = Buffer.concat([new Buffer([0x00]),
  patient_wallet.getPrivateKey()]).toString('base64')
let secKeyB = Buffer.concat
  ([new Buffer([0x00]),
   new_patient_wallet.getPrivateKey()]
   ).toString('base64')

exec('python3 ./generate_reEncKey.py ' + secKeyA + " "
  + secKeyB, (error, stdout, stderr) => {
  if (error !== null) {
    console.log(error)
  } else {
    let reEncKey = stdout.substr(2).slice(0, -2)

    console.log("Re-encryption Key for Patient's new
      Wallet: " + reEncKey)

    //Change patient's key
    let data = healthContractInstance.
      changePatientAccount.getData
      (reEncKey, new_patient_wallet.getAddressString(),
      new_patient_wallet.getPublicKey().
      toString('hex'));
    let nonce = web3.eth.getTransactionCount
      (patient_wallet.getAddressString())

    let rawTx = {
      gasPrice: web3.toHex(web3.eth.gasPrice),
      gasLimit: web3.toHex(4700000),
      from: patient_wallet.getAddressString(),
      nonce: web3.toHex(nonce),
      data: data,
      to: contract.address
    };

    let privateKey = ethereumjsUtil.toBuffer("0x" +
      patient_wallet.getPrivateKey().toString
      ('hex'), 'hex');
    let tx = new ethereumjsTx(rawTx);
    tx.sign(privateKey);

    web3.eth.sendRawTransaction("0x" +
      tx.serialize().toString('hex'),
```

```
                               function(error, result) {
                               if (error) {
                                 console.log(error)
                               } else {
                                 let events = healthContractInstance.allEvents({
                                   fromBlock: 0,
                                   toBlock: 'latest'
                                 });
                                 events.get(function(error, logs) {
                                   for (let count = 0; count < logs.length;
                                     count++) {
                                     console.log("Event Name: " +
                                       logs[count].event + " and Args: " +
                                       JSON.stringify(logs[count].args))
                                   }
                                 });
                               }
                             })
                           }
                         })
                       }
                     })
                   }
                 })
               }
             });
           }
         })
```

Here we created a sample EMR representing blood group. And then we put the hash on the blockchain and assumed putting the encrypted EMR on the Cloud server. And then we simulate a scenario where the Cloud server re-encrypts the ciphertext and the service provider decrypts the ciphertext. Finally, we generated another key pair and moved all EMRs of the patient to this account and closed the old account.

So, you saw how we simulated the whole user flow and how you can use PRE for security and privacy.

Summary

In this chapter, we learned how to use PRE for enabling encrypted data sharing in a blockchain. PRE can be a good alternative to private transactions and ZSL, in many cases. The architecture we looked at can be applied to many other use cases where sensitive assets need to be stored and shared among peers.

Apart from PRE, we learned about a lot of JS and Python libraries, such as `etherumjs-wallet`, `ethereumjs-tx`, `ethereumjs-util`, and `npre`. We also learned how to send raw transactions, such as the process of signing transactions using keys stored outside of the geth node. In the next chapter how to implement network permissioning in Quorum and how to build a solution to transfer money using a mobile number.

Building a Payment Solution for Banks

8

Today, there are lots of apps and services developed by banks and other FinTech companies that let us send and accept payments. But we don't have an app out there that makes sending and receiving money as easy as sending and receiving text messages. Although Bitcoin and other cryptocoins make it really easy to send and receive payments around the world, they cannot be mainstream now because of volatility and regulatory issues. In this chapter, we will build a P2P payment system that makes it very easy to send and receive **InterBank** payments and also makes clearance and settlement between banks near real-time and simple. While building the solution, we will also learn of various banking and finance concepts.

In this chapter, we'll learn the following:

- How clearance and settlement between banks is done for domestic and international InterBank electronic transfers
- How the **Society for Worldwide Interbank Financial Telecommunications (SWIFT)** system and international money transfers between banks work
- How to digitalize fiat currency on blockchains and the problems it solves
- How to implement network permissioning in Quorum
- How to build a solution to transfer money using a cell phone number

Overview of the payment system

In this chapter, we will build a payment solution to be integrated in mobile banking apps. This solution will let customers send payment using a cell phone number. Sending payments to anyone in the world using just a cell phone number would be the most friendly way to send payments.

Our solution will use digitalized fiat currency for the settlement and clearance of InterBank transfers. To understand why we choose to use digitalized fiat currency as the medium of settlement, let's understand how the settlement and clearance is done for InterBank transfers and its issues.

Settlement and clearance of InterBank transfers

Let's first understand how domestic InterBank transfers work. Every county's central bank has one more different types of centralized electronic fund transfer systems. For example, the **Immediate Payment Service (IMPS)** in India, **Automated Clearing House (ACH)** in the US, and **Electronic Funds Transfer (EFT)** in Canada. These systems are used by the country's banks to send messages to each other to facilitate the transfer of funds to their customers. It's only messages that are transferred, not real money. The final settlement happens through settlement accounts. Every bank holds a settlement account with the central bank, and money is either credited or debited in these accounts whenever there is a transfer message. To understand this more clearly, let's look at an example.

Suppose Bank A has a settlement account with the central bank with $50,000 credited to it. Similarly, suppose Bank B has a settlement account with the central bank containing $100,000. Now, say that X is a customer of Bank A and Y is a customer of Bank B. When X wants to send $100 to Y, Bank A sends a message to Bank B, via the fund-transfer system, indicating that it has debited $100 from $X's$ account and to credit $Y's$ account in Bank B with $100. After seeing this message, Bank B goes ahead and credits $Y's$ account with $100. To settle this payment, the central bank debits $100 from Bank $A's$ settlement account, therefore the new balance $49,900 and credits the settlement account of Bank B with $100 therefore making the new balance $100,100.

The central banks usually do the final settlements once a day at a specific time. The message transfers are near real-time. This process works fine as both banks involved trust the central bank.

Let's see how international InterBank transfers work. In this scenario, there are two banks of two different countries involved, and the way international payments work is different from domestic transfers. In the case of international payments, banks use the SWIFT system to send messages. SWIFT is a messaging network that financial institutions use to securely transmit information and instructions through a standardized system of codes. SWIFT assigns each financial organization a unique code that has either 8 or 11 characters. The code is interchangeably called the **Bank Identifier Code (BIC)**, SWIFT code, SWIFT ID, or ISO 9362 code.

To learn more about SWIFT, visit `https://www.investopedia.com/articles/personal-finance/050515/how-swift-system-works.asp`.

In this case, instead of having settlement accounts with a particular central bank, they have settlement accounts with each other. To understand this further, let's take an example. Suppose Bank *A* is a US bank and Bank *B* is an Indian bank. *X* is a customer of Bank *A* and *Y* is a customer of Bank *B*. To enable *X* to transfer money to *Y* and vice-versa, Bank *A* and Bank *B* hold settlement accounts with each other. So Bank *A* may have an account with Bank *B* with ₹300,000 credited and Bank *B* will have a settlement account with Bank *A* with $100,000 credited. Now, when *X* sends *Y* a payment worth $100, Bank *B* will debit ₹6909.50 (1 USD = 69.10 INR at the time of writing this book) from Bank *A's* settlement account that it handles. *X's* account will be debited for $100 and *Y's* account will be credited with ₹6909.50.

It usually takes five to seven days to reflect the credit in Y's account. It takes this is due to lot of necessary processes, checks, and issues, such as the following:

- As foreign remittance contributes to the money-laundering industry, banks have to do some sort of background check to establish that the funds you are using are not obtained from an illegal source.
- The sender's bank searches its system to check whether it has a direct partnership (holds settlement accounts) with the bank where the receiver's account is. Often it is unlikely. So, the sender's bank connects with a bank that they have a partnership with and also knows that the receiver's bank is also their partner. So essentially it becomes a chain. Sometimes, this chain can grow to three-four banks in the middle, depending on your country's banking infrastructure and the openness of its economy.
- Most of the time, these SWIFT messages are only sent by a single branch of the sender's bank that is designated to do foreign remittances. Also sender's branch will take some more time to send the message to that main branch and from there they will go ahead.
- In many countries, checks related to regulations and compliance are done manually, thus adding more time for the transfer to complete.

A **Nostro** account is the term used by Bank *A* to refer to our account held by Bank *B*. A **vostro** account is the term used by Bank B, where Bank A's money is being deposited.

Digitalizing fiat currency

We saw how InterBank transfers work. In the case of domestic transfers, the central bank has to take care of managing and updating the settlement accounts, whereas in the case of international transfers, the respective banks have to make the effort to update the settlement accounts. In the case of international transfers, there are other issues too, such as the requirement of more reconciliation effort, as there is no trusted third party, and the routing of payments through multiple intermediary banks.

Blockchains enable banks to transfer money to any other bank in the world directly by providing us the ability to digitalize fiat currency; it reduces the reconciliation effort by a huge extent by providing a single source of truth.

Let's look at the process and flow of digitalizing fiat currency on blockchain:

- Only central banks have the authority to issue their respective digitalized fiat currency on the blockchain.
- We can have a separate network for every fiat currency instead of using a single network to distribute traffic and increase scalability.
- For a bank to convert fiat currency to the digitalized form, it has to deposit fiat currency on the central bank's cash custody account. The equal amount of digitalized fiat currency will be issued to the respective bank by the central bank on blockchain.
- The bank can convert back digitalized fiat currency to paper currency at any time by destroying the fiat currency on blockchain.
- To achieve anonymity, banks can use multiple addresses. Therefore, it will be difficult for other banks to predict who owns how much digitalized fiat currency.

Using a cell phone number as identity

Our payment app will be based upon using a cell phone number as the identity of the receiver. Let's look at the whole process of using a cell phone number as the identifier of payment using a blockchain:

- The blockchain will act as a share-and-secured storage for cell phone numbers linked with the bank's code.
- Every ISD code will have its own network. This is done for scalability reasons.
- Every cell phone number can be linked to one or more banks. If there is more than one bank, the sender can select the bank account to which to send the payment.

- For a receiver to receive payments using a cell phone number, the cell phone number should be registered on the blockchain using the receiver's mobile banking app of the respective bank.
- If the receiver's bank account is suspended, the status should be updated on the blockchain to notify others not to accept payment for this cell phone number.

Building the network

Before we proceed to writing smart contracts, let's create Quorum networks for USD currency for the +1 ISD code. We will make sure that these networks are permissioned and protected using node IDs.

So far with, all the networks we have created in this book, we have assumed that they are protected using whitelisted IPs. But Quorum provides a way to whitelist node IDs. You can apply the same practice to other networks built in this book. A cell phone number shouldn't be leaked outside of the network, and therefore it's important to protect the network at all costs.

Network permissioning in Quorum

Network permissioning is enabled at the individual node level by adding the `--permissioned` flag as the command-line parameter during node startup. When the flag is added, the node looks for a file named `permissioned-nodes.json` in the node's data directory folder.

The `permissioned-nodes.json` file contains a list of node identifiers (`enode://nodeID@ip:port`) that this specific node will accept incoming connections from and make outgoing connections to.

If the `--permissioned` flag is set, but the `permissioned-nodes.json` file is empty, or is simply not present in the node's data directory folder, the node will start, but it will neither connect to any other nodes nor accept any incoming connection requests from other nodes.

For example, in our case, we need the minimum of a three-node network, that is, Bank *A*, Bank B, and the central bank. Suppose Bank *A's* node ID is `480cd6ab5c7910af0e413e17135d494d9a6b74c9d67692b0611e4eefea1cd082adbda a4c22467c583fb881e30fda415f0f84cfea7ddd7df45e1e7499ad3c680c`, Bank *B's* node ID is `60998b26d4a1ecbb29eff66c428c73f02e2b8a2936c4bbb46581ef59b2678b7023d30 0a31b899a7d82cae3cbb6f394de80d07820e0689b505c99920803d5029a` and the central bank's node ID is `e03f30b25c1739d203dd85e2dcc0ad79d53fa776034074134ec2bf128e609a0521f35 ed341edd12e43e436f08620ea68d39c05f63281772b4cce15b21d27941e`.

So the `permissioned-nodes.json` file on Bank A's node will have the following content:

```
[
"enode://60998b26d4a1ecbb29eff66c428c73f02e2b8a2936c4bbb46581ef59b2678b7023
d300a31b899a7d82cae3cbb6f394de80d07820e0689b505c99920803d5029a@[::]:23001?d
iscport=0",
"enode://e03f30b25c1739d203dd85e2dcc0ad79d53fa776034074134ec2bf128e609a0521
f35ed341edd12e43e436f08620ea68d39c05f63281772b4cce15b21d27941e@[::]:23002?d
iscport=0"
]
```

Similarly, Bank *B* will whitelist Bank *A* and the central bank, whereas the central bank will whitelist Bank *A* and Bank *B*.

Any additions to the `permissioned-nodes.json` file will be dynamically picked up by the server when subsequent incoming/outgoing requests are made. The node does not need to be restarted in order for the changes to take effect, but removing existing connected nodes from the `permissioned-nodes.json` file will not immediately drop those existing connected nodes. However, if the connection is dropped for any reason, and a subsequent connect request is made from the dropped node IDs, it will be rejected as part of that new request.

Building the DApp

Let's write the smart contracts for digitalizing fiat currency and storing cell phone numbers linked to bank accounts. Here is the smart contract for digitalizing fiat currency:

```solidity
pragma solidity ^0.4.18;

contract USD {
```

```
address centralBank;
mapping (address => uint256) balances;
uint256 totalDestroyed;
uint256 totalIssued;
event usdIssued(uint256 amount, address to);
event usdDestroyed(uint256 amount, address from);
event usdTransferred(uint256 amount, address from, address to,
  string description);
function USD() {
    centralBank = msg.sender;
}
function issueUSD(uint256 amount, address to) {
    if(msg.sender == centralBank) {
        balances[to] += amount;
        totalIssued += amount;
        usdIssued(amount, to);
    }
}
function destroyUSD(uint256 amount) {
    balances[msg.sender] -= amount;
    totalDestroyed += amount;
    usdDestroyed(amount, msg.sender);
}
function transferUSD(uint256 amount, address to, string
  description) {
    if(balances[msg.sender] >= amount) {
        balances[msg.sender] -= amount;
        balances[to] += amount;
        usdTransferred(amount, msg.sender, to, description);
    }
}
function getBalance(address account) returns (uint256 balance) {
    return balances[account];
}
function getTotal() returns (uint256 totalDestroyed, uint256
  totalIssued) {
    return (totalDestroyed, totalIssued);
}
}
```

This is how the preceding code works:

- We are assuming that the central bank deploys the smart contract.
- We have methods to issue, transfer, and destroy USD. These methods are self-explanatory. The transfer method also has a description that can contain information such as the purpose of the transaction or the receiving customer details.

- We have methods to retrieve the balance of an account, and the total USD ever issued and destroyed.

Here is the smart contract for holding the cell phone numbers and their respective banks:

```
pragma solidity ^0.4.18;

contract MobileNumbers {
    address centralBank;
    struct BankDetails {
        string name;
        bool authorization;
    }
    mapping (address => BankDetails) banks;
    mapping (uint256 => address[]) mobileNumbers;
    event bankAdded(address bankAddress, string bankName);
    event bankRemoved(address bankAddress);
    event mobileNumberAdded(address bankAddress, uint256 mobileNumber);
    function MobileNumbers() {
        centralBank = msg.sender;
    }
    function addBank(address bank, string bankName) {
        if(centralBank == msg.sender) {
            banks[bank] = BankDetails(bankName, true);
            bankAdded(bank, bankName);
        }
    }
    function removeBank(address bank) {
        if(centralBank == msg.sender) {
            banks[bank].authorization = false;
            bankRemoved(bank);
        }
    }
    function getBankDetails(address bank) view returns (string
      bankName, bool authorization) {
        return (banks[bank].name, banks[bank].authorization);
    }
    function addMobileNumber(uint256 mobileNumber) {
        if(banks[msg.sender].authorization == true) {
            for(uint256 count = 0; count <
              mobileNumbers[mobileNumber].length; count++) {
                if(mobileNumbers[mobileNumber][count] == msg.sender) {
                    return;
                }
            }
            mobileNumbers[mobileNumber].push(msg.sender);
            mobileNumberAdded(msg.sender, mobileNumber);
        }
    }
```

```
        }
        function removeMobileNumber(uint256 mobileNumber) {
            if(banks[msg.sender].authorization == true) {
                for(uint256 count = 0; count <
                    mobileNumbers[mobileNumber].length; count++) {
                    if(mobileNumbers[mobileNumber][count] == msg.sender) {
                        delete mobileNumbers[mobileNumber][count];
                        //fill the gap caused by delete
                        for (uint i = count; i <
                            mobileNumbers[mobileNumber].length - 1; i++){
                            mobileNumbers[mobileNumber][i] =
                                mobileNumbers[mobileNumber][i+1];
                        }
                        mobileNumbers[mobileNumber].length--;
                        break;
                    }
                }
            }
        }
        function getMobileNumberBanks(uint256 mobileNumber) view returns
        (address[] banks) {
            return mobileNumbers[mobileNumber];
        }
    }
}
```

Here is how the preceding code works:

- We assumed that the central bank deploys the contract.
- Then the central bank can add or remove banks to the network. Every bank gets an account on the blockchain. We cannot write a cell phone number using any account because that will let banks commit fraud—even if they don't own the account associated with a cell phone number, they will still add it and not get caught. A predefined account will enable audibility so that banks will not accept payments of a cell phone number whose account they don't hold.
- Then we have a method to add the cell phone number. Every cell phone number is associated with a lot of banks that the person has accounts with. At the time of sending payment, the sender can select one of these accounts.
- Then we have a method using which a bank can remove itself from a cell phone number. This is useful when the bank account is suspended or closed.
- Finally, we have a function to get list of bank accounts associated with a cell phone number.

Now let's see the whole flow of how a user payment and settlement would look:

- Assume *X* has an account with Bank *A* and *Y* has an account with Bank *B*. Both banks are registered on both networks, and both banks have sufficient amounts of USD on the USD network.

- For *Y* to receive a payment using a cell phone number, *Y* has to register its number on the MobileNumbers network using Bank *B's* cell phone number. Bank *B* will call the addMobileNumber method to register *Y's* bank account on the network.

- For *X* to send payment to *Y*, *X* has to enter *Y's* cell phone number into Bank *A's* mobile banking app. After that, Bank *A* will call the getMobileNumberBanks method to get a list of banks that *Y* has accounts with. Bank *B* will surely be listed, so *X* can select it and click the Send Payment button.

- As soon as the Send Payment button is clicked, Bank *A* will call the transferUSD method and provide *Y's* cell phone number in the description, indicating the bank account to credit the funds to. The to address in transferUSD will be the address returned by the getMobileNumberBanks method.

Summary

In this chapter, we learned some of the basic concepts of banking and how InterBank transfers are settled and cleared. We also learned about SWIFT and how it works. Then we jumped into advanced network permissioning in Quorum and learned about the -- permissioned flag.

Finally, we built a new type of fund-transfer system, which settles payment using digitalized fiat currency and a cell phone number for customer identification. We built the whole solution on a blockchain, which minimizes the reconciliation effort and solves lots of issues that it was not possible to solve previously.

Other Books You May Enjoy

If you enjoyed this book, you may be interested in these other books by Packt:

Hands-On Blockchain with Hyperledger
Nitin Gaur

ISBN: 9781788994521

- Discover why blockchain is a game changer in the technology landscape
- Set up blockchain networks using basic Hyperledger Fabric deployment
- Understand the considerations for creating decentralized applications
- Learn to integrate business networks with existing systems
- Write Smart Contracts quickly with Hyperledger Composer
- Design transaction model and chaincode with Golang
- Deploy Composer REST Gateway to access the Composer transactions
- Maintain, monitor, and govern your blockchain solutions

Blockchain Quick Reference
Brenn Hill, Samanyu Chopra, Paul Valencourt

ISBN: 9781788995788

- Understand how blockchain architecture components work
- Acquaint yourself with cryptography and the mechanics behind blockchain
- Apply consensus protocol to determine the business sustainability
- Understand what ICOs and crypto-mining are and how they work
- Create cryptocurrency wallets and coins for transaction mechanisms
- Understand the use of Ethereum for smart contract and DApp development

Leave a review - let other readers know what you think

Please share your thoughts on this book with others by leaving a review on the site that you bought it from. If you purchased the book from Amazon, please leave us an honest review on this book's Amazon page. This is vital so that other potential readers can see and use your unbiased opinion to make purchasing decisions, we can understand what our customers think about our products, and our authors can see your feedback on the title that they have worked with Packt to create. It will only take a few minutes of your time, but is valuable to other potential customers, our authors, and Packt. Thank you!

Index

Made in the USA
Middletown, DE
10 January 2019